Magnolias

Rosemary Barrett

Photographs Derek Hughes

FIREFLY BOOKS

A FIREFLY BOOK

Published by Firefly Books Ltd. 2002

First Printing

National Library of Canada Cataloguing in Publication Data

Barrett, Rosemary
   Magnolias
Includes index.
ISBN 1-55297-556-8 (bound)   ISBN 1-55297-555-X (pbk.)
1. Magnolias. I. Title.
SB413.M34B37 2002   635.9'77322   C2001-901801-0

U.S. Cataloging-in-Publication Data (Library of Congress Standards)

Barrett, Rosemary.
   Magnolias / Rosemary Barrett ; photographs by Derek Hughes. — 1st ed.
[96] p. : col. photos. ; cm.
Includes index.
Summary: Guide to using and growing magnolias in your garden.
Includes design ideas, sources and directory of magnolias.
ISBN 1-55297-556-8
ISBN 1-55297-555-X (pbk.)
1. Magnolias. I. Hughes, Derek. II. Title.
635.977322 21 CIP SB413.M34.B37 2002

Published in Canada in 2002 by
Firefly Books Ltd.
3680 Victoria Park Avenue
Willowdale, Ontario
M2H 3K1

Published in the United States in 2002 by
Firefly Books (U.S.) Inc.
P.O. Box 1338, Ellicott Station
Buffalo, New York
14205

Cover design Shelley Watson/Sublime Design
Design Errol McLeary
Typesetting Jazz Graphics, Auckland, New Zealand
Photographs by Derek Hughes
Printed in Hong Kong through Colorcraft Ltd

Page 1: The magnificent North American species *Magnolia grandiflora*.

Page 2: *Magnolia* x *soulangeana* 'Burgundy'

Page 3: Raised at the Arnold Arboretum in Boston, the splendid *Magnolia* x *loebneri* 'Merrill' flowers in profusion over a long period.

Opposite: *Magnolia* 'Sayonara'

Page 6: *Magnolia sargentiana* is named after Charles Sargent, a former director of the Arnold Arboretum in Massachusetts.

For my husband Rusty and my daughter Penny.

Acknowledgments

I would like to acknowledge the great and tactful help of my editor
Tracey Borgfeldt. My grateful thanks also to Derek Hughes and his partner
Anne Bayliss, without whose help this book would not have been possible.

Contents

Introduction

Why grow magnolias? Well, firstly, for their sheer beauty of flower. I do not think any tree approaches the breathtaking sight of a deciduous magnolia clothed from head-to-toe in flowers of arresting color and shape. Secondly, these trees are true aristocrats, with a stately bearing to match. Even without their marvelous flowers, they have a poise and charisma difficult to describe, but wonderful to behold. Thirdly, while many plants of special beauty can be difficult to grow, for example, some of the orchids, magnolias are blessedly simple in their requirements. Ernest Wilson, the great 20th-century British plant hunter, said of magnolias, "Their free flowering character and great beauty of blossom and foliage are equaled by the ease with which they may be cultivated."

With the new smaller-growing varieties, even tiny gardens can have at least one magnolia, and, if you choose carefully, and have the space to incorporate the wonderful American evergreen magnolia *Magnolia grandiflora*, you may have magnolia flowers over many months.

This is a book for hands-on gardeners, with practical advice and ideas from a gardener's viewpoint, rather than that of collectors, hybridists or nurserymen. I hope I can impart some of my knowledge and love of these wonderful trees to those who have not grown them before. And for those who already grow and love magnolias, I trust I can introduce you to some newer varieties that are particularly beautiful and rewarding. Of course, new hybrids appear all the time, some wonderful, some not so, but remember that there are still the tried-and-true magnolias that cannot be surpassed. We gardeners are extremely fortunate in that we have such a wide choice. Perhaps our only difficulty will be in deciding what to grow—but what a happy situation.

List of magnolia terms

Cultivar	a cultivated variety, a variety that has arisen in cultivation
Glaucous	a waxy coating that looks blue
Grex	a group of hybrids having the same two species as parents
Hybrid	offspring of two plants of same genus
Indumentum	hairs growing from underside of leaves
Leader	main growing stem
Precocious	flowering before the leaves appear
Species	plant found in wild, unlike any other
Sub	prefix meaning "almost"
Taxa	variety, species or genus
Tepal	magnolia petals
Variety	subdivision of a species; plants arising in the wild that differ from the species by some recognizable characteristic, but are not sufficiently different botanically to be designated a separate species

Hardiness Zone Map

This map has been prepared to agree with a system of plant hardiness zones that have been accepted as an international standard and range from 1 to 11. It shows the minimum winter temperatures that can be expected on average in different regions.

In this book, where a zone number has been given, the number corresponds with a zone shown here. That number indicates the coldest areas in which the particular plant is likely to survive through an average winter.

Note that these are not necessarily the areas in which it will grow best. Because the zone number refers to the minimum temperatures, a plant given zone 7, for example, will obviously grow perfectly well in zone 8, but not in zone 6. Plants grown in a zone considerably higher than the zone with the minimum winter temperature in which they will survive might well grow but they are likely to behave differently. Note also that some readers may find the numbers a little conservative; we felt it best to err on the side of caution.

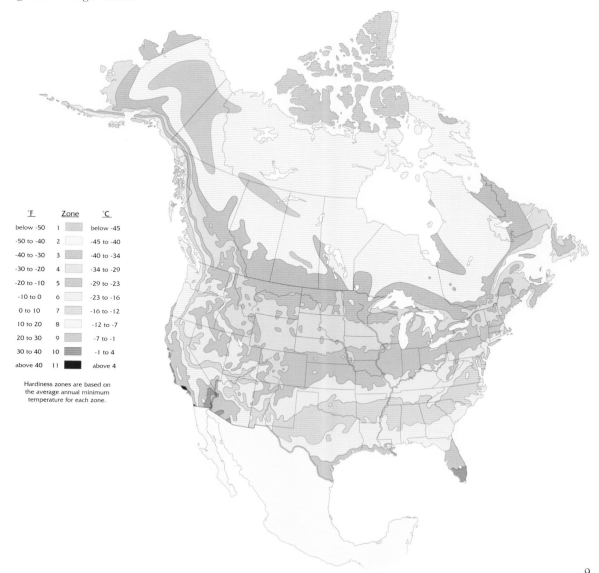

°F	Zone		°C
below -50	1		below -45
-50 to -40	2		-45 to -40
-40 to -30	3		-40 to -34
-30 to -20	4		-34 to -29
-20 to -10	5		-29 to -23
-10 to 0	6		-23 to -16
0 to 10	7		-16 to -12
10 to 20	8		-12 to -7
20 to 30	9		-7 to -1
30 to 40	10		-1 to 4
above 40	11		above 4

Hardiness zones are based on
the average annual minimum
temperature for each zone.

CHAPTER 1

Magnolias, their History

The When and the Where

I rather suspect that readers of gardening books skip the history of the genus in their haste to study the pictures and descriptions of the varieties. This is so they may choose what looks irresistible to them, and proceed to rush out to the nearest garden center. I have every sympathy with this attitude, but, all the same, knowing something of the history of the plant gives an understanding of how best to treat the new treasure, and also an appreciation of the efforts of intrepid plant hunters to provide these splendid trees.

Magnolias are like "Father Time," very old. Their fossilized remains have been found as far back as the Tertiary Period, which took place an unimaginable 100 million years ago. This makes them real survivors. We are very fortunate that this is so. I find it fascinating to read that at that time the Arctic Circle was not Arctic but European in climate, so that magnolias and associated plants, such as liriodendron and ginkgo, grew over a very wide area. Then there was a dramatic climate change, the polar ice cap expanded and the plants in the northern areas were destroyed. The plants of China, parts of Japan and eastern North America survived, however, and therefore have a great many similarities.

The name Magnolia commemorates a great French botanist, Pierre Magnol (1638–1715), who was known as an inspired teacher and a very prominent horticulturist. Because we are so accustomed

Opposite: A true breakthrough in color, *Magnolia* × *brooklynensis* 'Woodsman' was bred by Dr. Eva Maria Sperber at Brooklyn Botanic Garden.

to having such a diversity of plants from which to choose from, most of us do not spend much time thinking about just how they came to be ours to select.

When Pierre Magnol died in 1715 there was but one species of magnolia in Britain, then the epicenter of botanic development. This was the evergreen *Magnolia virginiana* from North America, known as swamp bay or sweet bay. It was sent in 1688 by a Virginian missionary called John Bannister, who had always been interested in botany.

These days *Magnolia virginiana* is not commonly grown by ordinary gardeners, perhaps because of the wide choice now available, but its creamy flowers have a sweet scent and it is smaller-growing than its relative, M. *grandiflora*, known as the southern magnolia, bull bay or great laurel magnolia. M. *virginiana*'s real importance is, perhaps, that it introduced Europe to a wonderful new genus, for neither evergreen nor deciduous magnolias are native to that continent.

After this, Sir Joseph Banks, who voyaged around the Pacific with Captain Cook in the late 18th century, introduced *Magnolia denudata* (Yulan magnolia) in 1780. But it was not until the 20th century that many of today's magnolias were introduced, in particular by two British men, namely George Forrest and Ernest "Chinese" Wilson. George Forrest was sponsored to go plant hunting by some wealthy European horticulturists, who then owned the plants he sent back. His adventures in China are better reading than the most gripping thrillers, because they are true. He said, "Living in

China is like camping alongside an active volcano." He had many horrific adventures, and was very tough and resourceful. He is remembered with gratitude for collecting thousands of plants, in particular, the wonderful M. *campbellii* subsp *mollicomata* and its marvelous cultivar 'Lanarth', which he took back home with him in 1904.

It is interesting to note that *Magnolia campbellii* itself was introduced in 1868 by Sir Joseph Hooker, who named it after Dr. Archibald Campbell, Political Resident at Darjeeling, India. These two magnolias of the same species differ in that *campbellii* subsp *mollicomata* comes from Yunnan province in China, and flowers a little later than does M. *campbellii*, which is from the Himalayas.

Ernest Wilson also introduced a great number of plants, including eight new species of magnolia. These beautiful species are widely grown today. They are *Magnolia dawsoniana*, M. *delavayi*, M. *officinalis*, M. *sargentiana*, M. *sargentiana robusta*, M. *sinensis*, M. *sprengeri* and M. *wilsonii*. From 1906 until his tragically early death in 1930, he worked for the Arnold Arboretum in Boston. No other plant hunter introduced so many species of magnolias.

Over the years, and up until the present day, plant hunters have, sometimes at very great risk, collected plants to save them from extinction, as well as to enhance the world's gardens. It is a tragedy that humankind so heedlessly destroys the environment to provide short-term benefit, so we should salute all plant hunters and their patrons. And let us not forget the gardeners themselves, who grow their plants, for their own pleasure no doubt, but even if not consciously, to both save and enhance our environment. To grow magnolias is an important part of this chain.

Once many species of magnolias had been introduced to Britain and North America, and rapidly also to other temperate climates, plant breeders set about producing beautiful hybrids from these species. The earliest of these hybridizers was a retired French army captain called Etienne Soulange-Bodin who in 1820 used *Magnolia denudata* crossed with M. *liliiflora* (syn M. *quinquepeta*) to produce *Magnolia* x *soulangeana*, a hardy old favorite still in gardens all over the world. There are at least forty selections of this particular cultivar grown today. What a splendid legacy from a man who was disgusted with the Napoleonic Wars, remarking that both sides would have been better at home planting cabbages. By this change in his lifestyle he did more to popularize magnolias as a garden subject than did the introduction of the original species.

Many very beautiful hybrids have originated, not from a plant breeding program as such, but from the efforts of dedicated gardeners, whether in making crosses or noticing chance seedlings of merit. Many truly magnificent hybrid magnolias have come from great British gardens, including some from the Royal Botanic Gardens at Kew in London (the superb 'Charles Raffill', 'Kew's Surprise'), Caerhay's Castle ('Caerhay's Belle', 'Caerhay's Surprise', *Magnolia sprengeri* 'Diva'), Nymans Garden (M. x *loebneri* 'Leonard Messel' and 'Michael Rosse'), Hillier's Arboretum, Bodnant and others.

In North America, the United States National Arboretum had a breeding program, starting in 1955, that made significant contributions. Under the auspices of Dr. Frances de Vos, *Magnolia liliiflora* 'Nigra' was crossed with M. *stellata* 'Rosea' to give us "the little girls," of which four were selected, and then, at the same Arboretum, Dr. William Kosar furthered the program, giving us another four. Magnolias 'Ann', 'Betty', 'Jane', 'Judy', 'Pinkie', 'Randy', 'Ricki' and 'Susan' are particularly useful in the smaller garden, growing to about 10 ft (3 m).

In 1956, at the Brooklyn Botanic Garden, Dr. Eva Maria Sperber bred some very interesting hybrids by crossing *Magnolia acuminata* with M. *denudata*. *Magnolia acuminata* (cucumber tree) is a very large deciduous tree with yellow-green flowers that come after the leaves and so tend to obscure these beautifully colored blooms. This species is

Above: The wonderful *Magnolia campbellii*, introduced to cultivation by the great plant hunter Sir Joseph Hooker.

used in breeding to try to produce yellow flowers on precocious magnolias (that is, those which produce flowers before the leaves come), therefore producing a much more spectacular display. The best-known hybrid from this cross is the lovely yellow-flowered M. 'Elizabeth'. Dr. Sperber then crossed M. *liliiflora* with M. *acuminata* to produce M. 'Eva Maria', which has purple tepals (petals in magnolias are always known as tepals) suffused yellow-green. This was a true breakthrough in color, a most exciting event. Twenty years later, J. C. McDaniel of Urbana, Illinois, produced the highly

Left: *Magnolia* × *soulangeana* is named after Etienne Soulange-Bodin, who did more to popularize magnolias through his early hybridizing than did the introductions of the early plant hunters.

regarded 'Woodsman', which has a mixture of yellow-green and purple coloring in the tepals. It is far more beautiful in reality than it is in description.

Other American breeders include Dr. Frank Galyon from Knoxville, Tennessee (*Magnolia* 'Paul Cook' and M. 'Emma Cook'), Dr. August Kehr of Hendersonville, North Carolina (M. 'Sundance' and M. 'Daybreak'), and Phillip Savage of Bloomfield Hills, Michigan (M. 'Big Dude', M. 'Marj Gossler' and the wonderful yellow called M. 'Butterflies').

Then there is Dr. Todd Gresham of Santa Cruz, California, who, coupled with Felix Jury of Taranaki, New Zealand, are to my mind the best magnolia hybridizers of all time. Dr. Gresham produced an unbelievable 15,500 hybrids, which were sent to various nurseries and evaluated by knowledgeable people. He has produced some of my very favorite

In 1780 Sir Joseph Banks introduced *Magnolia denudata*, the first Asiatic magnolia, to the west.

magnolias (which will be discussed in a later chapter), but magnolias 'Heaven Scent', 'Peppermint Stick', 'Sayonara', 'Manchu Fan', 'Rouged Alabaster' and 'Tina Durio' will ensure Todd Gresham a prominent place in magnolia breeding history.

Felix Jury is known worldwide for his splendid hybrids bred to flower at a young age—that is, at about only two to three years of age. Because of careful evaluation over many years, all these magnolias are very superior indeed and will be discussed in detail later in the book, but few magnolia lovers have not heard of magnolias 'Iolanthe', 'Serene', 'Vulcan', 'Lotus', 'Milky Way', 'Apollo', 'Athene' and 'Atlas'. Also in New Zealand, Oswald Blumhardt of

Important species of magnolia

There are about 125 species of magnolias, both deciduous and evergreen. The following list are some of the most important species in cultivation.

Species name (common name)	Place of origin	Height x width	Hardiness zones
M. *acuminata* (cucumber tree)	Eastern North America	70 x 30 ft (20 x 10 m)	4–8
M. *campbellii*	Himalayas	50 x 30 ft (15 x 10 m)	7–9
M. *campbellii* var *alba*	Himalayas	50 x 30 ft (15 x 10 m)	7–9
M. *campbellii* subsp *mollicomata*	China, Yunnan province	50 x 30 ft (15 x 10 m)	7–9
M. *cylindrica*	Eastern China	20 x 20 ft (6 x 6 m)	6–9
M. *dawsoniana*	Western China	50 x 30 ft (15 x 10 m)	7–9
M. *denudata* (lily tree, Yulan magnolia)	Central China	30 x 30 ft (10 x 10 m)	6–9
M. *grandiflora** (bull bay, southern magnolia)	Southeast United States	60 x 50 ft (18 x 15 m)	7–9
M. *kobus* (Kobus magnolia)	Japan	40 x 30 ft (12 x 10 m)	4–9
M. *liliiflora* (lily-flowered magnolia)	Eastern and central China	10 x 12 ft (3 x 4 m)	6–9
M. *macrophylla* (big-leaf magnolia, large-leafed cucumber tree, umbrella tree)	Southeast United States	30 x 30 ft (10 x 10 m)	6–9
M. *salicifolia* (anise magnolia, willow-leafed magnolia)	Japan	30 x 20 ft (10 x 6 m)	6–9
M. *sargentiana*	Western China	50 x 30 ft (15 x 10 m)	6–9
M. *sieboldii* (Oyama magnolia)	Southern China, Korea, Japan	25 x 40 ft (8 x 12 m)	6–9
M. *sinensis* (syn M. *sieboldii* subsp *sinensis*)	Western China	25 x 40 ft (8 x 12 m)	6–9
M. *sprengeri*	Central and western China	50 x 30 ft (15 x 10 m)	5–9
M. *stellata* (star magnolia)	Japan	10 x 12 ft (3 x 4 m)	5–9
M. *virginiana*** (swamp bay, sweet bay)	Eastern United States	30 x 20 ft (10 x 6 m)	6–9
M. *wilsonii*	Western China, Yunnan province	20 x 20 ft (6 x 6 m)	7–9

* = evergreen
** = deciduous or semi-evergreen (loses leaves below -17°F (-27°C)

Whangarei has bred some very good magnolias, the best-known being 'Star Wars', 'First Flush' and 'Early Rose'.

So, it can be seen that many dedicated, enthusiastic and knowledgable people have helped magnolias on their way.

CHAPTER 2

Cultivation

The How and the Why

So, you have purchased one or more magnolias (deciduous or evergreen) and need to know how to look after your new treasures. Well, the news is all good, for magnolias are very easy to grow. You would expect such aristocrats to be like racehorses, very temperamental, but not so. They need no particularly special treatment when planted and thereafter. Except for judicious pruning, and regular fertilizing, they are virtually carefree. Pests and diseases are relatively few (see page 21). The only downside is that they can be expensive to purchase, but I think you would be hard-pressed to find a gardener that regretted the expenditure. Little, if anything, surpasses the exquisite beauty of a magnolia bud, except the flower that follows.

Siting
Before planting anything, it is necessary to study the site that you think might suit. First of all, do what I often have not, and that is leave plenty of space for growth. Firstly so you get a specimen, not an amorphous mass, and secondly, if the trees are too closely planted the bottom branches die, which is not pretty. Another reason to be careful in your choice of site is that magnolias, with their spreading root system, do not transplant well, as much of the root system is lost during the move.

Magnolias like sun, so make sure they will get this benefit at least a good part of each day. Only the very large-leafed magnolias, such as *Magnolia*

macrophylla (zones 5–9) need part-shade. Most plants do not like strong winds, so avoid this curse, but other than this magnolias are not particular.

If your garden is sloping you are fortunate indeed, because magnolias may be planted on the slopes so that you look down upon them. I imagine that is how the early plant hunters saw them as they walked along ridges looking into the valleys of magnolia in flower. We can't quite manage such splendor, but in a small way we can replicate this beauty.

Planting
Magnolias like best to be planted in good, free-draining, preferably acidic (pH 5.0 to 6.5) soil that does not dry out, and they enjoy a sunny situation. However, *Magnolia kobus* (zones 5–9), M. x *loebneri* (zones 5–9), M. *seiboldii* (zones 6–9), M. *stellata* (zones 5–9) and M. *wilsonii* (zones 7–9) can grow in moist, alkaline soils and M. *delavayi* and M. *grandiflora* (both zones 7–9) will tolerate dry, alkaline soils.

As they like plenty of organic material in the soil, it is sensible to make a very good job of preparing the soil and site. Ensure that you dig a hole much larger than the root ball of the tree and add generous amounts of well-rotted manure and compost to enrich the soil. If your soil is dry, consider adding water-retaining crystals when you plant. These will expand to hold water when you water the tree after planting and give the roots a prolonged source of moisture to help them get established. It is not that magnolias are so fussy, it's just that you will be rewarded in proportion to the

Opposite: A soulangeana variety, 'Lennei' is both fast-growing and free-flowering.

17

Magnolia × *soulangeana* is probably the best known of all magnolias.

tend to girdle, that is, circle the trunk or root ball), gently tease the roots out from the bottom. Be careful doing this, because the roots are quite brittle. You can also cut any circling roots, espcially if they are at the top of the root ball or close to the trunk.

Make sure that the tree is firmly in the ground without actually stomping hard on it, and water well. I am a great believer in mulching your plant, being careful, as usual, to keep the material away from the stem to avoid stem rot. This is for more than one reason, the most important being to prevent the plant drying out. Depending upon what you use as mulch, and you have a wide choice, it can also provide nutrients. Suitable mulches are pea vine or barley straw (you do tend to get a crop of both peas and barley, but that is easily dealt with), bark, mushroom compost, leaf mold or compost.

If your plant is large, do stake it, because wind-rock can inhibit growth badly or kill the plant outright.

After-care

Having planted your tree, the after-care is not at all difficult. As magnolias are surface-rooting, do not use a fork vigorously or wield a mighty hoe, but do give them something to eat. Slow-release fertilizers are simple and good, and of course compost is wonderful. For the first year, it is necessary to make sure the plant does not dry out, but if you have mulched as suggested, the need for watering will be much reduced.

It is generally accepted that in these days of container plants you can plant them out at any time. This is not a theory to which I subscribe, unless you are the sort of person who will never forget to water when the season is dry. Fall is a good time to plant, for the soil is still warm enough to stimulate root growth. However, many magnolias are field-grown and therefore would not be lifted until early winter, so the plant you buy in the fall would be a holdover, perhaps getting very pot-bound. For this reason, I feel that spring is the very best option. Having

amount of effort you have expended. If you carefully prepare the site, your tree will grow more vigorously and therefore flower sooner. If the soil is poor, then the plant will look stick-like and grow but little a year. Eventually, however, it will flower.

Place your magnolia in the prepared hole, which should be about three times the width of the root ball, being very careful to plant it in the soil at the same level as it was in its container. If the plant has become root-bound in the pot (and magnolia roots planted, watered and mulched it, your magnolia can then be left to get on with growing without needing further attention for a while.

Coping with frost

If you plant your magnolias with regard to their recommended hardiness zones, they will flower successfully. However, whatever your climate, you may, in some years, experience late frosts, which can damage some flowers. Usually this affects only those species or cultivars that flower relatively early. The climate is unfortunately too variable to accurately predict the arrival of frosts in every year, so if you wish to grow the best of the Asiatic magnolias you are likely to have some years where frost damage will occur.

Having said this, there are some magnolias that shrug off frosts, e.g., *Magnolia stellata* and varieties and M. x *loebneri* and varieties, and so are ideal for those who live in areas where late frosts regularly occur. The other option is to choose magnolias that flower later in the season when frost danger is very low. Some suggestions are given in the list below.

Very late-flowering magnolias

M. *acuminata*, cultivars and hybrids: 'Butterflies', 'Elizabeth', 'Golden Glow', 'Goldstar', 'Koban Dori', 'Sundance', 'Yellow Fever'

M. x *brooklynensis*: 'Daybreak', 'Eva Maria', 'Woodsman', 'Yellow Bird'

M. *grandiflora* and selections: 'Beauty', 'Bracken's Brown', 'Charles Dickens', 'Edith Bogue', 'Exmouth', 'Ferruginea', 'Goliath', 'Majestic Beauty', 'Russet', 'St Mary'

M. *lilliflora*

M. *macrophylla*

M. *sieboldii*

Pruning

There are two schools of thought about pruning: one for pruning, one against—and wouldn't there be. If you are able to plant your magnolia with

Magnolias 'Sundance' and 'Ann' display lovely colors that work well together.

plenty of space around it, free-standing as it were, nothing looks better than a magnolia with its lower branches intact, so that the tree is clothed from head to foot.

However, life is full of compromise, so what I have found to be most practical is this: if you have to consider space, as most of us do, firstly keep the tree to one stem, where the variety allows. Then when the tree has grown, remove the lower branches up to a height of about 3 ft (1 m) or so.

Magnolia × brooklynensis 'Woodsman' marks a real breakthrough in magnolia colors.

This allows you to underplant, or should it be a lawn specimen, to mow with your "ride-on" without being beheaded. Pruning will not hurt the tree, but just watch for what are called water shoots (coming from where you cut) and simply remove them.

When it comes to species like *Magnolia stellata* and its hybrids (zones 5–9), which are naturally very bushy, it might be sacrilegious to suggest that you remove the lower branches so that you have a little tree rather than a shrub. This I have done and think it not only looks well and shapely, but saves lots of space. This is a big help in little gardens.

There are other reasons for pruning. Sometimes trees put up double leaders—that is, two leading or top growths. One will tend to be weaker than the other, so remove it, otherwise when the tree is older, a strong wind could break one leader. If the tree has branches that cross, they can rub together and cause damage and poor growth, so cut one out. Do this after spring flowering, pruning branches flush with the trunk. Also, be aware that magnolia branches are brittle and can break in ice storms, which is another good reason to prune weaker and damaged branches early.

Fertilizer

Magnolias in the wild grow in forested areas with lots of leaf mold for food. As we already mulched when planting, it will only be necessary to apply some slow-release fertilizer each year, in the spring and the fall.

If planted in a field situation, magnolias do not care for uncut grass growing around their trunks, so, if you can, mow around them or spray to prevent grass growth. In the garden, where your tree is probably underplanted, weed control needs to be different. As magnolias have roots very close to the surface, do not hoe, but remove weeds by some more gentle method, such as by hand.

Diseases and pests

Magnolias rarely suffer serious damage from diseases and insects. Very young plants can be attacked by slugs, but these pests are easy to control with modern baits. Sometimes, the leaves are attacked by leaf miners that chew through both leaves and flowers. This is especially a problem in the southern United States. Systemic insecticides will control these insects, but they are very toxic and, as the insects rarely kill the host plant, you may choose to live with the problem.

Another insect that might trouble your summer-flowering magnolia species and *Magnolia grandiflora* is the Japanese beetle. These can be picked off by hand, but in big trees and for large populations this is not feasible. If you live in a cold climate, winter will usually kill off these pests for you. Again, an insecticide can be used but you will want to weigh up the damage versus the use of chemicals to control the problem.

Other diseases that attack magnolias are leaf spots, including magnolia scab, and powdery mildew. Where you can reach the problem, spraying with a sulfur compound may help but often control is not needed or not practicable, especially on very large trees where good coverage is not possible. Various cankers, such as nectria canker, dieback and trunk decay can all be dealt with by cutting out the dead or diseased wood. Rarely will any of these diseases cause the death of the plant.

A far more serious problem is magnolia scale (*Neolecanium cornuparvum*). The scales are brown, round and about ¼ in (0.50 cm) in diameter. A white, dusty-looking wax often covers them. Like other scales, they suck sap from the plant and under continuous attack a tree may die. Excess plant sap is excreted as honeydew, on which the fungus sooty mold develops, giving the leaves and branches a telltale black appearance. Check for magnolia scale on any plant you are planning to purchase. If you see them on the plant, don't buy it.

If you find magnolia scale on your trees, you can apply horticultural spray oils (also known as summer oils) at all stages of the insect's life cycle. They kill primarily by smothering the scales and will be more effective if you first remove as many as you can by hand. These oils are most effective if you apply a horticultural oil to settled crawlers (the young of the insect) in late August. Then apply a dormant oil in October to November and again in March. Make sure that the stems and leaves are thoroughly wet.

Contact insecticides can also control scale, but the key to their success is timing. You need to apply sprays when the scale is at the crawler stage—usually late August to early September. (Crawlers are often orange, brown or purple and look like moving specks of dust.) Be sure to read the manufacturer's instructions carefully before using any oil or insecticide.

Other scale insects that attack magnolias include wax scales and tulip tree scales. Treat as for magnolia scale.

CHAPTER 3

Propagation

More from Little

It is usual in gardening books on a specific subject to devote a chapter to propagation, with diagrams and photographs of the progress of the young plant—a bit like a baby's progress book. I truly think, however, that the propagation of magnolias should be left to expert horticulturists. This, despite the fact that we have all heard about clever gardeners (or so they tell us) who just stick cuttings into shady soil and presto! a tree. This is not to say that people do not sometimes strike cuttings in this manner, but they are usually the common, easy subjects, and not choice magnolia cultivars.

Why this negative attitude? Well, because you need not only specialist gear but specialist knowl-

Magnolia campbellii 'Charles Raffill' is a beautiful magnolia and sadly beyond the scope of amateur propagation.

edge to propagate magnolias. For cuttings, you need bottom heat below and automatic mist spray above, although there are growing trays that are very useful for some plants and quite fun to work with. I strongly believe, however, that if you are serious about growing magnolias, don't spend your time and money unless you have all the right equipment and are ready to devote yourself to the outcome. After all, even if you do strike some magnolias that will grow from cuttings, you will have to wait a very long time before your plant equals the one you can buy from your garden center. If it is a variety that will actually grow from cuttings, then the chances are that when you select it from the nursery or garden center, it will very likely be in bud, or at the very least planning to flower the following year. Your homegrown plant, on the other hand, will be about three years behind.

Cuttings

For those who are dedicated to "doing it yourself" and are not bothered about the timeframe, this is what you must do. In early mid-summer, when the new growth has hardened a little, take a cutting of new growth where it joins last year's hardwood. Remove all but three or four leaves, then reduce the remaining leaves to about half their size. This prevents excess water loss, and also enables more cuttings to fit into the tray, which will have been filled with a suitable commercial propagating mix, watered and firmed down. Dip the cutting into a rooting hormone powder and place in the tray. Keep damp. Wait.

Magnolia × *soulangeana* will grow reasonably readily from cuttings.

When the cuttings are rooted, and this will take between three and six months, pot the plants and place them in a shadehouse or such a shelter, until they have recovered from the shock. When they start to make new growth, plant them in the vegetable garden or other cultivated space and let them grow on until large enough to be planted permanently in the garden. This will take at least a year.

Seed

Growing magnolias from seed is a truly long-term hobby, but you could perhaps be rewarded with something special. If you sow seeds of species they will come true, but if the seeds come from hybrids, who knows what you might get? You will notice that many magnolia seed pods are rather spectacular, brightly colored "cucumbers." When the seed is ripe—that is, when the fruiting cone splits—collect and dry the fruits. When dry, but not desiccated, shake the seeds free and put them in a bowl of warm water to which you have added 1 tsp (5 mL) of dishwashing detergent. This is to remove not only the hard outer coating but also the oily film. Take out of the water and place seeds in the refrigerator until late winter/early spring. Then prick in the seeds in a tray containing suitable seed-raising mix. Wait. How long can be very variable indeed. When the seedlings are big enough, pot them, then proceed as for cuttings.

Budding and grafting are very skilled methods of propagating, so if you aspire to this, you will likely need some lessons from a professional. This is, of course, perfectly possible, but usually beyond the scope, or perhaps even interest, of everyday gardeners.

CHAPTER 4

Landscaping with Magnolias

The Art of Beautification

It seems to me, and just maybe I'm biased, that any garden can best be enhanced by the addition of a magnolia. Do not be timid, even if you have a small garden. You might only be able to plant one tree, but remember, if you choose a suitable plant then the base does not require much room and the rest is up in the air. It can then be underplanted with all sorts of low-growing plants, such as bulbs, perennials and shrubs, and will provide a sheltered microclimate for them. However, be careful if you want to use groundcovers, as they tend to smother as well as cover and compete with the magnolia's roots for nutrients and moisture.

Of course, you need to think of the tree's eventual height and make sure it only blocks a view that you don't want to see. Then year-round, it will provide you with interest, from the delectable woolly buds through winter to the much-anticipated flowering, the quiet green of summer, and in some varieties, but not all, lovely fall color. It is often suggested that smaller-growing species, like *Magnolia stellata* (zones 5–9), are suitable, and so they are, especially if, as has been previously suggested, you trim them up 3 ft (1 m) or so. But you need not be so limited, as you can trim your magnolia to the height you wish.

For those with small gardens

These days a great many people have small, or very small, gardens. This doesn't necessarily preclude

Opposite: A specimen magnolia like this *Magnolia × soulangeana* can become a focal point for the garden.

them from growing magnolias, for although it is obvious that the taller *Magnolia campbellii* (zones 7–9) is not for them, there are other very beautiful magnolias that can be accommodated. The first thing is do not be timid, for a garden without a tree is just decoration around the house, with no real focal point, no height, no atmosphere—at least, that is what I think.

The best magnolia for small gardens is the species *Magnolia stellata*, as it is small-growing with delicate star-shaped flowers in either white or pink. Normally this magnolia is not a tree, but rather a very bushy shrub. This limits our options, but with judicious pruning it can be turned into a small tree by removing the lower branches so that underplanting, particularly of bulbs, can take place (see page 30). For a white magnolia I consider 'Waterlily' the best choice, as the beautifully scented flowers have more petals than the species *stellata*. For pink my choice is 'King Rose', which comes out flushed pink then fades. An American clone called 'Jane Platt' is a richer, deeper pink. These *stellata* are hardy to zone 5. 'Royal Star', another white, has a hardiness rating of zone 3.

If your garden is very tiny, perhaps you might have to settle for just one of the magnolias mentioned above, but it will reward you by flowering for a long time and from a very young age. Magnolias can be grown in pots (the Japanese do this), but I personally do not recommend it, as it reminds me too much of bonsai. If all you have is a courtyard with a raised bed, *Magnolia stellata* could fill a corner and even provide a little shade.

(3–4 m). They are very attractive and very hardy (zones 3–8). They are 'Ann', 'Betty', 'Jane', 'Judy', 'Pinkie', 'Randy', 'Ricki' and 'Susan', and all are very pretty, colored red-purple and scented. My favorites are 'Ann', which looks quite spectacular with the sun shining through it, luminous and beautiful, and 'Pinkie', which has flowers paler than the others and completely smothering the tree. The "Little Girls" flower over a very long period, which makes them particularly desirable.

The magnolias I have chosen so far have small flowers. Still bearing in mind the constraints of a small garden, there are some larger-flowered but not large-growing magnolias that would be very suitable. Carefully sited, these trees can block a less-than-beautiful view or, more positively, add height and elegance to your garden.

There are not many "white" magnolias that are pure white, but a slender tree that is to die for is called *Magnolia* 'Suishoren' (zones 6–9). It is very generous with flowers, mannerly and attractive, and I strongly recommend it. In the same desirable

Above: *Magnolia stellata* 'King Rose'
Right: The delightful *Magnolia sieboldii* has nodding white flowers with bright red bosses of stamens.

For a small garden that is not absolutely tiny, the *Magnolia* x *loebneri* cultivars are absolutely splendid. 'Leonard Messel' (25 x 20 ft/8 x 6 m) is perhaps my all-time favorite with its star-like flowers that are pink on the outside, white within. It flowers over many weeks, is not bothered by frost (hardy to zones 5–9) and has very acceptable fall color. An American cultivar of great merit is 'Merrill' (zones 5–9), flowering when very young in a most prolific manner.

The U.S. National Arboretum produced something called the "Little Girls." These are *Magnolia stellata* x M. *liliiflora* hybrids that grow to 10–12 ft

category is M. 'Pristine' (zones 6–9) bred from that all-time favorite M. *denudata* by Professor McDaniel of Illinois. The flowers are smaller than those of M. *denudata*, very dainty and appealing.

Something a little different and very suitable for small gardens is the delightful species *Magnolia sieboldii* (25 x 40 ft/8 x 12 m). This treasure has nodding, pendulous, white flowers with bright red bosses of stamens. The fragrant flowers are produced over many weeks and then intermittently for another month or so. It is hardy to zones 6–9.

From these few suggestions it can be seen that, though your garden be small, if you have a mind to grow at least one carefully selected magnolia, it is possible, not to mention desirable, to do so.

'Pinkie' is one of the "Little Girls" and is very generous with its flowers.

Small-growing magnolias
20 ft (6 m) or less
M. 'Ann'
M. x *loebneri* 'Leonard Messel'
M. x *loebneri* 'Merrill'
M. 'Pinkie'
M. 'Pristine'
M. 'Suishoren'
M. *seiboldii*
M. *stellata* 'Jane Platt'
M. *stellata* 'King Rose'
M. *stellata* 'Waterlily'

For those with large gardens

There is, of course, more scope in the larger garden. If you are starting with a blank canvas, magnolias will do very well in cultivated beds. As you no doubt are planning to grow other genera, it means that your magnolias will be nicely separated, making splendid specimens, and as it is said that magnolias like company, other trees and shrubs will mix and mingle very well.

As well as blending into the mixed border, magnolias can also be used to telling effect as a lawn specimen, making a focal point for the whole garden. As it is important to use your garden, not just toil in it, this tree can provide a delightful place in which to sit in the shade enjoying the particular pleasure of outdoor living, sipping an evening wine while dinner cooks on the barbecue.

If you live in the country and have some land, or even a whole farm, you have a wonderfully large canvas with which to work. Groups of one variety look especially splendid, because you get a greater visual impact with the larger mass. It is usually suggested that such groups be in uneven numbers, e.g., three, five, seven, etc., because then the group will look informal rather than regimented, which would not be suitable in this type of planting. If you had, say, 10 acres (4 ha) and used about nine groups of trees in whatever sized groupings from three upward, your field would look splendid and this would not be too ruinously expensive to implement.

To me, however, a large garden is anything above about 1 acre (0.4 ha). This size enables you to grow a fair number of magnolias, if you wish. As usual, it will be a matter of personal choice, but the choice offered is very wide and you no doubt will want both large- and small-growing magnolias.

I would recommend at least one *Magnolia camp-bellii* (for reasons given in chapter 5, For Those Who Can Wait: The Patient Gardener). The one I would choose is M. *campbellii* subsp *mollicomata* 'Lanarth' (50 x 30 ft/15 x 10 m), because the color is both gorgeous—deep deep magenta—and differ-

Above: *Magnolia* 'Star Wars' looks splendid in this country setting overlooking the still waters of a lake. Opposite: 'Apollo' and 'Athene' are both at home in a rural setting.

ent from any other magnolia. If you could manage two, how about M. *campbellii* 'Darjeeling' in dark purple crimson? So you want three? Add M. *campbellii* var *alba* 'Strybing White'. All are hardy in zones 7–9.

You have to wait up to five to seven years for these beauties to flower, so it is an excellent idea to choose some magnolias that will flower almost as soon as you purchase them. See chapter 6, For Those Who Cannot Wait: Instant Gratification, for some wonderful choices.

You cannot go wrong choosing Gresham or Jury hybrids; even the most particular gardeners will be

delighted with these lovely trees. Their heights vary from 20–30 ft (6–10 m) and they are hardy to zone 6. I find it difficult to suggest which of these hybrids I prefer, but here goes. I would dislike being without the following, all of which flower at a very young age (if they are not in bud when you purchase them, they will almost certainly flower the following year): 'Vulcan', 'Tina Durio', 'Apollo', 'Sayonara', 'Lotus', 'Sweetheart', 'Manchu Fan' and 'Elizabeth'. You could manage even more.

In the section above covering small gardens, my favorite smaller-growing magnolias are discussed and, of course, the large garden has scope for a good many of these. Do not overlook any of the varieties of *Magnolia stellata* and the larger, but still "small", "Little Girls" from the U. S. National Arboretum, or M. 'Pristine' and M. 'Suishoren'.

In the shade

Should you be lucky enough to have, or be planning, a woodland garden, magnolias are absolutely ideal to provide shade. Deciduous trees are what you need, as once the leaves fall, the winter sun can sweeten the soil. I have to admit that magnolia leaves are very leathery and take a long time to break down, so you might want to rake them up and compost them, and then return them to the soil as a mulch.

The woodland garden should be a quiet haven without much wind, with trees making dappled shade and all sorts of treasures growing in their beneficial shelter. The magnolia fits into that environment like a hand into a glove, making the early spring a glory, flowering before other deciduous trees, like maples, have come into lovely leaf, then

Above: Magnolias 'Lotus' (left) and 'Galaxy' are ideal for shade in a woodland garden.
Right: Bulbs, particularly daffodils and bluebells, make a splendid spring display with *Magnolia* 'Ann'.

returning into a leafy background until, with the turn of the seasons, the furry buds provide winter interest. Some magnolias, for example *Magnolia loebneri* 'Leonard Messel' (zones 5–9), have good fall color, too, but most unfortunately do not.

Courtyard gardens

Some houses have courtyards especially designed to be outside rooms where relaxation in the open air is much prized. Often these courtyards incorporate raised beds where plants, particularly those that are scented, can grow. There would be place in this case for *Magnolia stellata* or varieties (zones 5–9) that have lovely perfume and can be easily clipped to shape and size. If that is not feasible, these small-growing trees can be accommodated in very large

pots. They need to be filled with a potting mix suitable for magnolias (available from garden centers), watered regularly, and given mulch and slow-release fertilizer that can be applied to the surface.

Companion planting
Underplanting

You have planted magnolias in beds or perhaps in the lawn, or in the surrounding fields should you be so fortunate to have access to such space. As magnolias do not like to have their roots disturbed, many of which are close to the surface, I favor the use of bulbs to underplant trees growing in the lawn or field, especially bulbs that are happy to naturalize. Daffodils and bluebells are splendid for spring display, making a delightful composite picture with the magnolias flowering above. I would then leave it at that—beautiful, trouble-free and attainable, requiring no further attention than an annual tidy-up.

Above: *Magnolia* × *soulangeana* 'Lennei Alba' is a splendid feature in this courtyard garden.
Left: Choice bulbs for underplanting are trilliums and frittillarias—both are elegant and beautiful.

In the woodland garden, which is of course cultivated, you have a wide range of choice bulbs and plants. To herald spring you could have firstly the trillium, or the wood lily, sometimes known as the wake-robin. These native North American woodland plants, with their leaves and flowers all in threes, as the name "*trillium*" suggests, are elegant and beautiful, and require both damp and shade. It cannot be emphasized enough that it is necessary to rake off fallen magnolia leaves, as they do not break down quickly and could smother small, delicate bulbs. Daffodils and bluebells planted in fields under magnolias, however, are quite strong enough to look after themselves.

While the trilliums are still flowering, for their season is very long, another woodland treasure comes along, the frittillarias, with nodding bells of modest mien and subtle charm, often checkered and with some unusual colorings. The common, but just as beautiful as any other, species *Frittillaria meleagris* would naturalize quite happily if left to itself under the light shade of magnolias.

The delightful erythronium, so unattractively called the dog's-tooth violet, fits in beautifully with the other bulbs mentioned. These little treasures are also native to North America and come in shades of pink, yellow and white. They are easy to grow, increase with alacrity, and have not only lovely delicate-looking but quite hardy flowers, but also beautifully mottled leaves. I find them quite irresistible.

Cyclamen are also quite happy to grow under trees. They are dainty and most beautiful and, what's more, they can flower over many months. *Cyclamen hederifolium* flowers in the fall and *C. coum* in the late winter into spring. They may be planted close to the magnolia trunk, where the soil tends to be drier, because they don't mind being dry. When cyclamen are not in flower, you have their truly beautiful, often marbled leaves to study.

Cyclamen coum, and other cyclamen species, are happy to grow under magnolias.

And what about hellebores? Undemanding, flowering through winter into spring with subtle colors and modestly hanging heads, the *orientalis* hybrids are easy plants for under trees. Another very common woodlander, of which I am particularly fond, is Solomon's seal (*Polygonatum multiflorum*). Bold clumps of its lovely, arching stems with their white, bell-shaped flowers, tipped green, look just wonderful under trees, and they will spread very satisfactorily. They are strong and unfussy and would just love to be sheltered by a magnolia.

Finally, let us not forget the strange and strangely beautiful ariseama, looking faintly evil, often with striped trumpets and lovely leaves. They are truly different and their subtle beauty grows on you. There are all sorts of other plants to underplant magnolias, but these are my very favorites and I commend them to you.

A note on groundcovers

It is better in my opinion to avoid groundcovers under your magnolias, as they can be very invasive. Also, although they are supposed to suppress weeds, and to a certain extent they achieve this, once weeds get in (and they inevitably do), the groundcover can then make them extraordinarily difficult to eradicate.

Flowering shrubs

It is said that all magnolias like company. I often wonder which magnolia told which botanist this. However, as magnolias grow among other trees in the wild, this is no doubt true. The role of shrubs would be very adequately filled using kalmias, rhododendrons and camellias, and mollis (deciduous) azaleas. They all enjoy the same soil and growing conditions.

Kalmia

Kalmias grow in zones 6–9 and reach a height of 6 ft (1.8 m). They are beautiful flowering shrubs native to North America, whose flowers can be pink, red,

Kalmias like 'Sarah' are flowering shrubs that are native to North America and good companions for magnolias.

white or bicolored. Flowering in the early summer, they do not flower at the same time as most magnolias (which flower in the spring), and so do not compete with magnolias for attention. The plant has a graceful shape and the buds, and then the cupped flowers, provide a wonderful display. Their buds are so beautiful that if they never opened into flowers, the plant would still be very well worth growing. I particularly favor 'Ostbo Red' (pink), 'Pink Frost', 'Sarah' (red), 'Carousel' (bicolor) and 'Stillwood' (white).

Rhododendron

Rhododendrons, with their wide range of colors and flowering times, make excellent companion plants for magnolias. Those of us who live in zone 6 and warmer can grow the rhododendron species *maddenii*, with its scented white flowers often with a yellow throat; *Rhododendron polyandrum*, which shows the same attributes; and *R. nuttallii* and its crosses with *R. lindleyi*, which are divine. But if you live in colder climes do not despair, for there are so many others that you can grow, from the magnificent *R. grande* down through all sorts of hardy hybrids. Your best plan is to go to your local garden center or nursery and pick what you fancy.

Camellia

Camellias are beautiful in leaf, stunning in flower and there is a very wide choice of varieties. Growing well in zones 6–10, camellias start flowering in the winter and continue into spring. They are splendid complementary plants with colors that blend very well with those of magnolias. It is good, too, that they are generally trouble free and do not need a lot of fuss. I favor the very beautiful species *Camellia reticulata* and its many hybrids for their large flowers and because the shrub has a graceful habit. There are literally hundreds of camellias to choose from and a spring visit to your garden center means that you can select them while in flower. This allows you to see what varieties will blend most pleasingly with your magnolias.

Azalea mollis

I am very fond of azalea mollis, which are deciduous shrubs covered with myriad flowers in spring, sometimes in very bright colors and often perfumed. As an extra dimension, they sport lovely, colored leaves in the fall.

Rhododendrons and magnolias go well together. Here, *Rhododendron* 'Van Nes Sensation' is flowering just as *Magnolia* 'Pinkie' is displaying its last flowers.

When the magnolias are waning, there isn't a more beautiful sight in the garden than *Cornus florida* 'Cherokee Chief' in full flower.

Rosa rugosa

Another choice of shrub which might not immediately spring to mind, but that I think is to be recommended, is the shrub rose, specifically *Rosa rugosa*. This is a species that does not require spraying, is very hardy, and has simple, but simply beautiful, single, perfumed flowers in colors of white, pink, red and purple. There are many desirable hybrids of this species, and most have stunning hips in the fall. They don't require much in the way of pruning, just a bit of a haircut occasionally.

Trees

The choice of trees as companions for your magnolias is very wide, and while the choice is yours, I must say I favor deciduous trees for this task. Their display is not static but incorporates bare branches and beguiling buds in winter, lovely emerging leaves in spring, and glorious fall color. I shall mention a few of my favorites.

Cornus

The first of these is flowering dogwood, the wonderful native North American *Cornus florida* (zone 5–9) and its cultivars. These are small trees (height 15–20 ft/4.5–6 m) that have beautiful "bracts" that look like wide-open flowers of simple design, in colors of white, pink through pinkish-red, to red. They are most delectable and adorn the tree's bare branches for many weeks. Then in the fall comes a truly glorious display of colored leaves—from reds, through oranges to yellows, depending on the cultivar. As some cornus have variegated leaves, the fall display is even more spectacular because the variegation means more variety of colors on each tree. In winter, the little knobby buds remind you that spring's flowers are not too far away.

It is best to buy named varieties, because they will be superior and because seedlings often take many years to flower; while the cultivars should flower within a year or so. For white "flowers", i.e., bracts, try 'Cloud 9' and 'Cherokee Princess'; for pink, 'Spring Song' and 'Stokes' Pink'; and for red, 'Cherokee Chief' and 'Rubra'. If you like variegated leaves that have stunning fall color, try *Cornus* 'Cherokee Rainbow', 'Cherokee Sunset' or 'Cherokee Daybreak'. These cornus are wonderful in their own right, and wonderful companions to magnolias.

Maples

Another excellent, small (15–25 ft/4.5–7.5 m) tree to keep your magnolias company is one of my all-time favorites, the Japanese maple—*Acer palmatum*, *A. p. dissectum* and *A. japonica* species and cultivars (zones 6–10).

These trees are special because they are so graceful and hardy and because their spring leaves rival in color the truly splendid fall display. The emerging leaves are exquisite, delicate and subtle, holding their color for a long time before turning to quieter summer colors. In fall, the stunning blaze of color seems almost unreal. Whichever variety, they are all beautiful, so it is just a matter of personal choice, and as I love them all (but some a little more than others), I shall just mention a few of my very favorites. For red-toned leaves I would suggest *Acer palmatum* 'Shindeshojo', 'Osakazuki', 'O'Kagami' (a particularly strong grower), 'Sherwood Flame', 'Fireglow' and the truly special, small-growing 'Beni-Komachi'.

For incredible, almost fluorescent spring greens, it would be difficult to pass by *Acer palmatum dissectum* 'Seiryu', the only upright form with delicately cut leaves, and also *A. p.* 'Katsura'. The latter is green in the summer but with the palest yellow leaves touched with orange and red tints in the spring.

There are also variegated Japanese maples, should such be to your taste. A favorite of mine is *Acer palmatum* 'Shigitatsu Sawa', which is an elegantly shaped, small tree with pale green leaves showing prominent tan veins. *A. p.* 'Orido Nishiki' is very striking because its leaves are variegated bright pink with cream margins. *A. p.* 'Asahi Zuru' is similar, very small and fancy. There are so many from which to choose that it is best to go to your local garden center or nursery, where you can decide which are for you.

The universally beloved weeping maples would also be just as splendid alongside or in front of your magnolias. They come in red, green or variegated colors, on standards of various heights.

All these delightful maples are to be strongly commended as companion plants. Just remember that, although they are hardy, they cannot abide much wind, so site them accordingly.

Betula

Out of the huge range of deciduous trees, one of the loveliest has to be *Betula*, the birch. There are many varieties of birch and all have in common the fact that they are graceful and elegant, with a light and delicate leaf canopy, leaves that are soft green in spring, gold in the fall, and stunningly beautiful bark. They would look very well among magnolias.

The scarlet fall leaves of *Acer palmatum* 'Osakazuki' show up vividly against the green of *Magnolia grandiflora*.

Betula pendula make especially beautiful specimen trees for larger gardens.

Just remember that they are very greedy and so need regular feeding to prevent their robbing nutrients from surrounding plants.

A choice smaller deciduous tree is the American redbud, *Cercis canadensis* 'Forest Pansy'.

Cercis

A choice, smaller tree (18–20 ft/5.5–6 m) is the redbud, *Cercis canadensis*, one of North America's finest deciduous trees. The very best selection is 'Forest Pansy', which has outstanding heart-shaped, wine-red leaves. Its fall colors are splendid, light in tone in oranges and reds. You would be missing endless pleasure and excitement if you failed to grow this lovely tree. It would fit in most any garden. The redbuds flower a little later than most magnolias.

There are a great many desirable deciduous trees, but those that I have mentioned are what I most recommend as companions for magnolias, particularly for smaller gardens.

Companion trees for the large garden

Just because you have a larger garden does not mean that you have to fill it with plants of noble dimensions. Rather, it just means that you may do this if you wish, and it also means that you can have groups of one variety. It also means, lucky you, that you can have an eclectic mix of companionable, large trees to keep company with your magnolias. You might even have a field and be able to plant a "park," just trees and groundcover or grass.

What trees to select to complement your magnolias? The choice is large and we will at least pretend that this mythical garden is of ample dimensions. If, in fact, you cannot manage all that is suggested, then once again it is a matter of choice.

The long spring months are filled with the glorious flowering of the Asiatic magnolias and the sweetly scented flowers of *Magnolia grandiflora* enhance summer. Fall, then, which does a splendid job of providing color with leaves instead of flowers, is the season on which to concentrate.

Think first of yet another wonderful North American native, the *Liquidambar styraciflua* or sweetgum (zone 6). This lovely tree is quite unrivaled for the splendor of its fall color. The rather large leaves are maple-like, and the tree itself has a pyramid shape, so it is handsome and striking at all times. It is similar to magnolia in liking the soil to be reasonably damp while abhorring strong winds, but in the fall it takes center stage, and even Japanese maples are not any more beautiful.

We are fortunate not to have to rely on species trees whose fall colors can disappoint, but instead can choose from a wide range of varieties. I have a very soft spot for *Liquidambar styraciflua* 'Aurora', because over the fall it turns the most amazing, psychedelic colors—yellow, orange, red and purple all on the one leaf. This selection comes from Australia, as does the flamboyant 'Kia' in red, orange and purple. You could have 'Burgundy', a North American variety, its fall leaves are wine-red, deepening to purple and staying on the tree longer than usual. Another splendid North America selection, 'Palo Alto', comes in orange and red in the fall, and the spring and summer leaves in green are also most attractive. 'Worplesdon' is very graceful, because

A mixed collection of magnolias.

the branches are a little pendulous and the fall color is lighter than other varieties, in lemon, apricot and pale orange. The last variety I know well is 'Lane Roberts' and its fall color is very dark, a black crimson-red.

If you have room plant them all, for they are splendid trees, but at least plant one or two. It will not be only you who will be rewarded, for these trees will provide pleasure for those who follow you.

The golden-yellow fall foliage of *Fagus sylvatica*, the common beech or European beech (zones 5–10) is, I think, one of the most beautiful of all fall displays, and then there is what is commonly called the copper beech (*F. s.* form *purpurea*). The selected form 'Riversii' turns bronze-colored in the fall, then a lovely, soft tan. These are some of the noblest of the famous English trees, and you are fortunate indeed if you can accommodate them.

Ginkgo biloba (zones 5–10), a tree of ancient lineage, has the most glorious fall color. Its fan-shaped leaves are oddly attractive at all times, but they are a wonder to behold in the fall. Do not grow a female tree, for the fallen fruits have a very foul odor. 'Fairmount' is a very good male form.

Another very ancient tree with outstanding fall color is *Metasequoia glyptostroboides* (zones 5–10), commonly known as dawn redwood. Its history is romantic, because comparatively recently (before the 1940s) it was thought to be extinct, found in modern times only as a fossil. Then, amazingly, it was discovered growing in a remote area of China. *Metasequoia* is a deciduous conifer with lovely, soft green, fern-like leaves and its fall foliage is just beautiful in a soft, golden tan. It likes to be reason-

Magnolia × *soulangeana* 'San Jose' as a roadside tree.

ably damp and looks very well beside water. Another deciduous conifer that is very similar and equally as desirable for our palette of fall color is *Taxodium*, or swamp cypress (zones 5–10). The great difference is that this tree will actually grow *in* water, however, it is just as well suited to any good soil. Its fall color is a rich shade of chestnut. These two conifers make a very good contrast with the more usual fall color of most deciduous trees.

As we have all that space in our large garden, we should certainly have at least one oak. *Quercus* (zones 4–9) come in both deciduous and evergreen forms, but for our purposes we are interested in just the deciduous. My very favorite oak is *Quercus palustris* (30–40 ft/9–12 m), commonly called pin oak. It is another beautiful native of the eastern United States, with a very graceful habit of growth and finely cut leaves that turn red, yellow and russet in the fall. But, I think this a quite outstanding tree at any time of the year.

My second favorite oak is also North American: *Quercus coccinea*. Its fall color is the most amazing crimson-scarlet. Beware, however, this tree gets pretty big (50–60 ft/15–18 m) and few home gardens are large enough to accommodate it.

Sorbus aucuparia (known commonly as rowan or mountain ash) is another large tree (50 ft/15 m) and in the fall it makes a very loud statement, for it not only has vivid orange-red to rich gold leaves but delectable red berries. It is very hardy (zone 4), but really needs the fall to be cold to color well.

We are inclined to think of ornamental cherries as trees we grow for their glorious spring blossoms, but it is not altogether so, for they have the most beautiful fall colors. Many flowering cherries are from Japan, the home of so many beautiful plants, and they generously provide us stunning flowers followed by fall color of yellows, oranges and reds. They grow in zones 6–9 and reach 15–20 ft (4–6 m).

Nyssa sylvatica (black tupelo, sour gum, pepperidge) is a relatively tall tree (60 ft/21 m) from the eastern United States that has gloriously bright fall colors in shades of orange and scarlet. It is special and another favorite of mine. It is hardy to zone 5.

CHAPTER 5

For Those Who Can Wait

The Patient Gardener

Many of us, partly because of age and partly from impatience, want flowers on our magnolias yesterday. Let us not be short-sighted, however, for many of the aristocrats of the magnolia world take some years to flower. But how worthwhile the wait, and how very great the reward. I do not suggest, of course, that you have only these slow-maturing types, but rather an eclectic mix of both precocious and slow is ideal.

Magnolia campbellii is universally known as the "queen of magnolias," and rightly so. It is magnificent in both size (up to 115 ft/34 m) and poise, and the startling beauty of its huge, pink, fragrant blooms is unsurpassed. This species comes from the

Himalayas, and, not to be confusing, it has a subspecies, M. *campbellii* subsp *mollicomata*, that comes from the Chinese province of Yunnan. The subspecies is basically the same as M. *campbellii*, but it differs in that the flowers come later in the spring, and flowers at a younger age than the species.

Magnolia campbellii flowers in late winter and so can catch the lingering frosts, which *mollicomata*, by flowering about three weeks later, can miss. However, should you live in a zone colder than 7, your

Above: *Magnolia campbellii* 'Charles Raffill' is a splendid variety whose bright pink flowers come later in the season than other *campbelli*.

Magnificent in both size and poise, *Magnolia campbellii var alba* is startling in its beauty.
Opposite: *Magnolia* 'Darjeeling'

tree could suffer both flower and leaf damage, thus the species and subspecies are not for you. For those who can grow this noble tree, I urge you to do so, even if one is all you can manage.

Do not buy seed-raised *Magnolia campbellii* because they may take twenty years to flower, and, as with all seedlings, the color could be variable. They are cheaper to buy, but do not be tempted. Buy a grafted plant of a named variety and you get exactly what you expect. Into this category comes 'Landicla', a gorgeous, deep pink fading to a paler pink as the flower ages, and 'Darjeeling', outstandingly beautiful in a dark wine color.

You would, I think, also love to grow the white *campbellii*, *Magnolia campbellii var alba*, if your climate suits. It flowers early in the season, really when winter still has a grip. It is just lovely, not a pristine white, but flushed gently with greenish-yellow at the base of the flower. Even more spectacular, to my mind, is the cultivar M. *campbellii var* 'Strybing White' whose outer tepals hang down in a most attractive manner.

When it comes to selected forms of M. *c.* subsp *mollicomata*, 'Lanarth' is truly superb. The flower is a deep magenta that fades with time. The shape is of the characteristic cup-and-saucer of the magnolia, and is the epitome of elegance and beauty. *Magnolia* 'Charles Raffill' is a very splendid form, too, with bright pink flowers that arrive later than either M. *campbellii* or M. *c.* subsp *mollicomata*, its parents.

Another species that requires patience is *Magnolia dawsoniana* (zones 7–9). Its red-suffused white flowers hang limply in a rather attractive, raffish way that is not to everyone's liking. 'Chyverton Red' is a more spectacular color, and there is a form that I have not seen, called 'Clarke' that is red-pink on the outside, paler inside. This form has the great advantage of flowering at a comparatively younger age, about six years. It originated at Clarke Nursery in California, hence its name.

If you are not at all in a hurry, purchase the absolutely choice *Magnolia sprengeri* 'Diva', truly a goddess among magnolias, brought back from a plant-hunting expedition by Ernest "Chinese" Wilson. The cup-shaped flowers are a stunning rose-pink, streaked darker on the inside. It is just beautiful and deservedly very popular in North America, because it is hardy up to zone 5. One of its offspring is called 'Burncoose', a deep pink-purple, and there is 'Claret Cup' and 'Copeland Court', all in varying pinks. These plants will take about ten years to flower, but once they start to flower they produce a very generous display each spring.

Another lovely but slow-to-flower magnolia is *Magnolia sargentiana* (zones 7–9), named after Charles Sargent, director of the Arnold Arboretum in Massachusetts, who saved many of "Chinese" Wilson's magnolias by sending all the young plants to the kinder climate of France to be propagated. It grows very large (80 ft/24 m) and has pink flowers, a bit like M. *dawsoniana*. *Magnolia sargentiana* 'Robusta' has a very interesting habit: it has rose-red flowers that open in a nodding position then bend over to present their full faces.

CHAPTER 6

For Those Who Cannot Wait

Instant Gratification

Jury hybrids

Felix Jury was a small man with a large vision. He was not formally trained in horticulture but, rather, was a farmer with an avid interest in plants. His tastes were catholic, but I think that in the end he will be remembered best for the magnificent magnolias he bred on his Waitara farm in Taranaki, New Zealand. He wanted garden-worthy magnolias that would flower at an early age, and he succeeded magnificently.

Felix established himself as a camellia breeder of international standard and then in the 1960s turned to magnolia breeding. He thought he imported *Magnolia* 'Lanarth', which turned out not to be so, but was probably a hybrid between 'Lanarth' and M. *sargentiana* var 'Robusta'. He subsequently named this beautiful plant 'Mark Jury' after his son. Today, Mark, with his wife Abigail, carries on the business and continues his father's breeding program.

Magnolia 'Mark Jury' is a great personal favorite of mine, with huge pink flowers that have a hint of lavender. As Graham Rankin, author of the splendid book, *Magnolia: A Hamlyn Care Manual* (1999), remarked, "It was fortunate that this seedling ended up with someone who was so admirably capable of utilizing it to its full potential."

Felix Jury quietly worked away, and in the early 1970s released perhaps his most famous magnolia, the noble 'Iolanthe'. Like all the others he bred, it flowers when very young (only two years), its flowers are large and its furry buds quite enormous. The Jury hybrids are all hardy to zone 6. It should be remembered that magnolia buds are a splendid addi-

Above: The lovely 'Iolanthe' is hybridizer Felix Jury's most famous magnolia. It has enormous furry buds.
Opposite: *Magnolia* 'Atlas'

tion to this plant's attractions and there are none more attractive than the huge, hairy buds of 'Iolanthe'. The flower color is always given as pink, though I feel that it has a distinct lavender or light purple tinge. There are a tremendous number of flowers, as it is a most generous tree and an unforgettable sight in full bloom. If I had a criticism, I would say that the flowers are perhaps a little too large, which makes them a tad floppy, but 'Iolanthe' is a wonderful cultivar nevertheless and highly regarded worldwide.

A sister seedling is called 'Atlas'. Its flowers are simply enormous (15 in/38 cm across) and a rather pretty, soft pink. It is really for people who think

Above: 'Serene' flowers over a long period.
Right: 'Vulcan' at its best is breathtakingly beautiful—its color luminous and its shape a dainty cup-and-saucer.

looks "pinky" rather than "milky." Nevertheless, the flowers sit along the branches in a most poised and attractive way and it is scented.

I have a particular fondness for 'Serene', which has rounded blooms of a color somewhere between purple and carmine pink. It is scented and flowers over a long period. Its name very aptly describes its poise.

Magnolia 'Lotus' is a beauty, so named because its shape, when wide open, looks like a water lily. Of course, it is white. It does not flower quite as young as the other Jury hybrids, but it is well worth the wait—which is still short compared to so many other magnolias. If I were forced to choose just one Jury magnolia, I think it would have to be the lovely 'Lotus'.

Having said that, what about one of the most talked about of Felix Jury's creations, the extraordinary 'Vulcan'? At its best, it is unsurpassed as far as

bigger is better and certainly makes a shouting statement. You need a large garden to accommodate 'Atlas', not because the tree itself is so large, but just to keep things in proportion. It would smack of treason to place it in the shrub border. I think that because of its splendidly large flowers it could be called a "man's plant" (aren't women supposed to like "namby-pamby" plants, i.e., smaller and daintier?), but whatever your taste, it is surely an achievement to produce a plant with the largest flowers of any Asiatic magnolia hybrid.

If you want a class act, Jury's 'Athene' is most certainly a contender. The flowers are scented, white with a basal pink flush and in full bloom there would scarcely be room for another flower. What's more, this wonderful display happens at a very young age (2 to 3 years). For sheer beauty and abundance, I do not think this hybrid magnolia can be easily surpassed.

Then from the same stable comes the lovely 'Milky Way', which is white with a pink base, so it

Above: The scented pink and white flowers of 'Milky Way' sit along the branches in a very attractive way.

the splendid-colored, early-maturing hybrids go. The color is a rich ruby red, but the catch is that when the tree is young the flowers tend to be a disappointing mucky purple, as are often the late-season flowers on the mature tree. Notwithstanding, 'Vulcan' at its best is breathtakingly beautiful, the color luminous, the flowers not too big, and held in classic cup-and-saucer shape, but daintily so. It has to be said that in my quite large collection it is the most admired.

Magnolia 'Apollo' is a sister seedling to 'Vulcan' and because it is bred from M. 'Lanarth' x *liliiflora*, it has inherited wonderful color, a truly lovely violet-purple outside and white inside. A mere description does not do justice to this magnolia, which is so fresh and crisp, and generous (as are all the Jury hybrids) with the amount of flowers. No variable color here; it is always totally reliable.

Mark Jury has recently released the next generation of Jury hybrids. The first is called *Magnolia* 'Black Tulip' and it is a truly outstanding color, a very dark ruby red showing as nearly black. This flower seems to me to lack importance, as it seems

small for the size and stature of the tree. However, as it gains maturity (my tree is just three years old), the goblet-shaped flowers might not look so stumpy—a little elongation of the petals would make all the difference.

Then there is a magnolia that certainly cannot be criticized for lack of size: 'Felix Jury' (syn 'Flamingo'). I have always said that I did not like flowers to be too big, but this new magnolia is magnificent and in time will certainly receive world-wide recognition. The color is a very acceptable red, as in magnolia red not fire engine red, and the flowers are very large indeed. This magnolia is awe-inspiring and a fitting tribute to a breeder of so many splendid plants. I would not be without it.

Above: Stunning in both color and size, 'Felix Jury' may well be the best of the Jury hybrids.

Lastly, one magnolia not yet released, and likely to be called 'Ruby Star', is very different from the others mentioned, but I think has great charm. It is a narrow tree and it has a narrow, upright flower of real elegance. The color is very dark, ruby red, hence its name. It will make a great contribution to magnolias of this desirable color, but it is still being evaluated, not for color, but to assess its ability to flower continuously. Something to look for in the future.

It seems remarkable to me that the Jury hybrids are all such outstanding plants and it is difficult to choose between them. I think the only solution to this dilemma would be to grow them all. Certainly, if you were starting a garden and did not want to wait very long for the flowers, this would not be a silly suggestion.

Gresham hybrids

Felix Jury produced a limited number of splendid hybrids and lived to see them flower. In the United States in the 1950s, Todd Gresham, who was a founding member of the American Magnolia Society, embarked on a very ambitious and, as it turned out, very successful project. Over forty years later, we who love magnolias are still enjoying the results of his dedication and expertise. He did not live to see all his splendid hybrids flower, but they all flower at a very young age and many experts think that these plants offer an improvement on the ever-popular *soulangeana* hybrids.

Dr. Gresham "painted on a very large canvas" and produced a quite enormous number of seed-

lings. He very sensibly sent hundreds of these to carefully chosen nurseries for evaluation. I can well imagine the excitement when they flowered, and the agony and anxiety of separating "the sheep from the goats," so to speak. But the people chosen to do that were experts, so the plants that have been named are the true cream of the crop. As with the Jury hybrids, the Gresham magnolias are known and cherished all over the world, tailored to the needs of most of us who appreciate the fact that as gardeners we hope not to be in our dotage before seeing the flowers.

Of course, with so many seedlings produced from the same crosses, only a small proportion will be outstanding, so when you purchase a Gresham hybrid you know you have the very best out of thousands. This gives you great confidence that even if you are buying on description alone, you can buy in the sure knowledge that experts have considered these named hybrids as excellent.

The choice is delightfully wide and all are vigorous. This attribute I think is very important so that you know your plant is not a subject needing special care. The Gresham hybrids are medium-sized trees (20–25 ft/6–8 m), hardy in zones 6–9 and all flower mid-spring, though this can vary depending on your particular climate.

Some of the most appealing Gresham hybrids are white with flushed bases. I think my very favorite has to be the divine 'Tina Durio', which has quite large cup-and-saucer-shaped flowers in the *campbellii* tradition, with just a little pink at the base. It has a particularly serene beauty, perhaps because white is not a shouting color, and it is perfumed.

Then, coming close behind in my popularity stakes is 'Sayonara'. This magnolia is fast-growing and its fragrant, white flowers are goblet-shaped, tinged pink-purple at the base. The erectly held blooms have real poise and presence.

Left: The lovely buds of 'Tina Durio'.

Above left: Rather like *Magnolia denudata*, 'Manchu Fan' has tepals of a texture thicker than normal.
Above right: 'Heaven Scent' is an early Gresham hybrid that flowers prolifically.
Right: The most striking attribute of 'Peppermint Stick' is its wonderful erect, elongated buds.

'Manchu Fan' is a white-flowered hybrid with a purple stain at the base and is rather like the ever-beloved *Magnolia denudata*, but with thicker-textured petals. It has the great advantage of flowering later in the season, which is handy for dodging frosts. The flowers of 'Manchu Fan' are smaller than the other white Gresham hybrids, which I certainly do not see as a fault, and they are both elegant and perfumed, making this hybrid very desirable.

'Rouged Alabaster' is not much different from 'Manchu Fan', except that its pink-tinged white flowers are very large and bloom early in the spring. Once again, they are fragrant, which most of us find very acceptable indeed.

Magnolia 'David Clulow' is a recent arrival to my garden and I am eagerly awaiting its flowering. It is like a smaller version of M. *campbellii* var *alba* and there cannot be a higher recommendation than that. It is said to be one of the very best white magnolias in cultivation, which, when you consider the opposition, is very high praise. I hope that Dr. Gresham lived to see this outstanding achievement in flower.

The charmingly named 'Sweet Sixteen' has tapered pink buds that open in great profusion into pure white, cup-shaped flowers. White-flowered Gresham hybrids, with which I am not familiar but which are highly regarded, include 'Eliza Odenwald', '14 Karat' and 'Mary Nell'. In due course I certainly hope to own these also.

There are also some delightful pink Gresham hybrids. For many years we have had great pleasure from the aptly named 'Peppermint Stick', which is called white-suffused-pink, but the general effect is pink-and-white. Its most striking attribute is the wonderful, elongated buds that sit along the branches in the most attractive way. When the flowers open they are perfectly acceptable but not particularly distinguished; the buds are this tree's prize.

Magnolia 'Heaven Scent' is an early Gresham hybrid that flowers very prolifically. The color is a rather attractive lavender; however, there was something a little too creative in the naming of this very garden-worthy magnolia, because for the life of me I cannot smell any scent, heavenly or otherwise.

Magnolia 'Joe McDaniel', named after a former president of the American Magnolia Society who was a professor of horticulture, is very fine, its color a striking pinkish-purple. It has large, goblet-shaped flowers.

A Gresham hybrid that flowers early in the season (i.e. before mid-spring) is 'Royal Crown'. It bears dark reddish-purple, tall flowers and has the very pleasing habit of flowering over a long period. It is not to die for, and perhaps you would not buy it if you had to be very selective, but, unlike most of us, it grows in beauty with age, making a grand display in maturity.

Magnolia 'Joe McDaniel'

'Todd Gresham' was named for the breeder of all these stunning American hybrids, so it is fittingly very handsome with flowers that are red-purple outside, white within. I think all magnolia lovers should own it, not only for itself, but to remind us of a man of such vision and dedication that he has left us a legacy of outstanding hybrids, many, many more than are mentioned here. I cannot talk about all of the Gresham hybrids because I have not seen them all—a situation I hope to remedy in time. Both Felix Jury and Todd Gresham can be bracketed together as quite outstanding magnolia hybridists. We owe them—for beauty of flower and, very importantly, for allowing us, if not instant gratification, certainly the closest thing to it.

CHAPTER 7

The Soulangeana Hybrids

A Soldier's Achievement

A French cavalry officer, Etienne Soulange-Bodin, returning home from the Napoleonic Wars, was disgusted at the carnage and reportedly said, "It had doubtless been better for both parties to have stayed home and planted their cabbages. We are returned here and the rising taste for gardening becomes one of the most agreeable guarantees for the repose of the world." And so from 1820 onward, he raised the hardy magnolia hybrids we have loved for all these years, known as *Magnolia* x *soulangeana*, a cross between M. *denudata* and M. *liliiflora*. It is commonly accepted that by doing this, M. Soulange-Bodin did more to popularize the genus *Magnolia* than did the plant hunters who introduced the species. Perhaps this does not seem quite fair, since the plant hunters risked a great deal in often very hostile environments, but I think they must in fact be regarded as a partnership. Without the original introductions no hybrids would have been possible.

And what splendid hybrids they are. There are today still about forty "soulangeanas" in cultivation from just the one original cross, which speaks volumes for their quality (the balance are no longer regarded so highly). The reason is that they are beautiful, they are hardy, and they flower at a young age. Hybridists following this clever Frenchman made the same cross, the result being that we now have many to choose from. Not surprisingly, some are a little too similar to each other, but you can

have flowers ranging from pure white to deep purple that can be cup-and-saucer-, goblet- or tulip-shaped. They have proved very easy to cultivate and only a comparatively few years back were the only hybrids commonly seen in gardens. In fact, they have reigned supreme for 170 years or so and only very recently, with the introduction of the splendid Gresham hybrids from North America, have they been challenged. We as gardeners are so fortunate to have such a huge selection. It makes one long for untold acres, and a hired gardener or two to go with them.

Where to start? As these magnolias are not forest giants, but rather multi-stemmed shrubs that will grow into small, broad, spreading trees (approximately 20 x 20 ft/6 x 6 m), they are eminently suitable for most gardens, especially if you remove the lower branches to provide room for underplanting (see page 19). This is just being practical, for although I think magnolias flowering literally from top to toe are as they really should be, this is not always a manageable option. As tribute to M. Soulange-Bodin, I would first suggest *Magnolia* x *soulangeana* itself (syn 'Etienne Soulange-Bodin'). The cup-and-saucer flowers are white inside, flushed pink on the outside with purplish-pink at the base. It can hold its own with any magnolia, and is always a joy in full bloom. *Magnolia* x *soulangeana* and its hybrids are hardy to zones 5–9.

Next, I would suggest *Magnolia* x *soulangeana* 'Alba' (syn 'Alba Superba'). This is truly delicious, with white flowers flushed pinky purple at the base. Another white that can certainly be called 'superb'

Opposite: 'San Jose' is a very fine soulangeana from California.

'Picture' has tall, elegant buds and large flowers.

is M. x *soulangeana* 'Lennei Alba', with its thick-textured white flowers and so lovely that it was used by both Felix Jury and Dr. Todd Gresham in their breeding programs. *Magnolia* x *soulangeana* 'Lennei' has strongly rosy purple flowers that are white inside. It is a late-season flowerer, which is an advantage where late frosts are more likely. It, too, has been used in modern breeding programs, proving its quality.

There are about a hundred named *Magnolia* x *soulangeana* selections, including the forty or so 'originals' from M. Soulange-Bodin, and although many are not readily available, there are still plenty to recommend. *Magnolia* 'Grace McDade' is a North American cultivar with very large flowers of creamy white with a purplish flush. Its growth habit tends to be sprawling, so you need to use your loppers from time to time, and judiciously.

The famous Sawadas Nursery of Japan introduced the very popular 'Picture', which is different from the other soulangeanas in that it has very large flowers from tall, elegant buds. The flowers are very dark purple at the base fading to pink and are white within.

'Rustica Rubra' is a well-loved variety that has rose-purple flowers with white interiors. It is pleas-ant without being "over the top," but perhaps its best attribute is that it is darned hardy and so very useful in difficult situations.

'San Jose' is a very fine variety from California that generously displays its hundreds of pink flow-ers, which are white inside, in the greatest abundance. It is one of the joys of early spring but therefore subject to sneaky, late-spring frosts. It is also delightfully scented.

Magnolia 'Alexandrina', from the same stable, is deservedly popular, with a scented flower that is tulip-shaped, white flushed with purple on the outside and white inside. 'Brozzoni' from Italy is considered one of the very best cultivars, pure white with the slightest hint of pink, cup-and-saucer-shaped (eventually) and late to flower. This not only escapes an untimely frost but, in combination with other magnolias, also extends your magnolia flowering season. The season of magnolia flowering is so special, so filled with excitement and anticipa-tion, that any plant that extends this wonderful time is a treasure.

Magnolia 'Burgundy'—such a nice plain name, telling you in one word what to expect—was raised by W. B. Clarke of San Jose, California, who also introduced the splendid and aptly named M. 'San Jose'. It is interesting to read how light conditions in different countries affect the color of flowers. 'Burgundy' is just that in North America and New Zealand, but in Britain it is a sort of rose-pink. I guess this partially explains the disappointment of British gardeners with Mark Jury's M. 'Vulcan'. I have seen a photograph in J. M. Gardiner's book *Magnolia's: A Gardeners Guide* that shows my favorite M. x *loebneri* 'Leonard Messel' as a wishy-washy pink, because day and night temperatures had been very cold during spring. The accompany-ing photograph in this book, taken in a milder year, shows it as it should be (see page 64).

Magnolia 'Speciosa' has flowers that are nearly white, but with slight pinky-purple tones. It is not as readily available as other soulangeanas but is a very

Above: A well-loved variety, 'Rustica Rubra'.
Left: *Magnolia* x *soulangeana* 'Lennei Alba' has been used extensively for breeding programs.

attractive plant that flowers towards the end of spring.

Magnolia 'Verbanica' is another soulangeana, and is widely grown. It has pleasant cup-shaped flowers in a strong pink. It shares the attributes of the others soulangeanas in that it is hardy, free flowering and will grow almost anywhere. Anyone starting a garden featuring magnolias would be well advised to choose at least one or two soulangeana hybrids, not only for the above attributes but because they are also very beautiful. You would also be growing a very important part of magnolia history, commemorating a man who did so much to popularize magnolias and provide gardeners with plants that could be enjoyed in flower in a very short time.

CHAPTER 8

To Die For

The Best in White

Where not so many years ago the choice of magnolia varieties was restricted, you did not have to agonize too much about what to plant; nowadays, the situation is very different, with wonderful new cultivars appearing frequently, backed up by stunning introductions over the last few years. So how to choose? Of course, beauty is in the eye of the beholder, so different people like different plants, but over the next few chapters I am going to share what I consider to be the cream of the offerings, starting with white.

White flowers always seem to me to be special. Perhaps it is the purity of color, the serenity white provides and certainly the contrast with other more "shouting" colors is important, but, however it may be, white is just a fabulous color.

In the very early spring (and if you still experience frosts at this time, this is unfortunately not for you), one of the most exciting events of the year is the flowering of *Magnolia campbellii* var *alba* and the form known as 'Strybing White' (both zones 7–9). *Magnolia campbellii* is pink and takes a number of years to flower, but the white versions are a good deal swifter to produce their spectacular flowers.

Most of us want instant flowers—who wouldn't? —but we can afford to have one or two that will take a much longer time. While you admire those that flower in just a year or two, you will know that there are stars waiting in the wings. They will not have to wait backstage too long if you are careful in your purchases. Make sure that you buy a grafted (or

Opposite: Magnolia campbelli var alba 'Strybing White'

chip-budded) plant where *Magnolia campbellii* subsp *mollicomata* has been used as rootstock. This cuts the waiting time in half.

In the still wintry-looking landscape of very early spring, *Magnolia campbellii* var *alba* is a wonderful sight, standing tall and serene and smothered in white flowers, marking the retreat of winter and the happy advance of spring. If a tree can be said to have a spiritual quality, this is surely the one. It flowers without competition from others, so you have time to study and appreciate it, a rewarding experience.

'Strybing White', a distinct form, differs from the usual *campbellii* cup-and-saucer flower shape in that the saucer droops instead of being flat. Some people do not like this, but I think it very attractive. It is named after the Strybing Arboretum in San Francisco. Two other cultivars that are white and very fine are 'Ethel Hillier', which has very large flowers that have a pink tinge, and 'Maharanee', a delightful pure white.

While these lovely trees are quietly growing in the background, center stage might well be taken up by *Magnolia denudata*, the lily tree hailing from China (see page 11), and planted by Buddhist monks in their temples as long ago as the 6th century. It was the first Asiatic magnolia introduced to the West (in 1780 by Sir Joseph Banks) and remains one of the most popular worldwide. I suppose this is because it is so absolutely beautiful, the pure white flowers simple and elegantly held, very refined and aristocratic. It will fit into almost any garden, for it is really just a large shrub or small tree. Like M.

Magnolia denudata 'Purple Eye'

campbellii var *alba*, late frosts can mar the flowers, so it is best to choose a sheltered site if you do sometimes suffer late frost. It is not that M. *denudata* is not hardy, for it is rated zone 5, but most flowers can be affected by frost. Like the white *campbellii*, *denudata* has a special, serene quality, and should you be able to provide a dark background, for example, with conifers, the sight of the tree in full flower is unforgettable. It also smells just lovely.

Magnolia denudata 'Purple Eye' (zones 5–9) is a hybrid with very large white flowers with a distinct purple flush both inside and outside the tepals. Of course, it is lovely, but it does not have quite the

refinement of *denudata*. Having said that, I still would not be without it. It is quite a vigorous grower.

A species, of which for some reason I did not expect too much, has with age simply delighted me. It is *Magnolia salicifolia*, commonly known as the willow leaf magnolia, from Japan. Perhaps because its leaves are skinny, not like those of other magnolias, I somehow thought the flower wouldn't be much. Certainly they are not large, but there are so many of them that they smother the tree in a shimmering white cloud. It flowers for simply ages and is seductively scented. It is quite large-growing (30 x 20 ft/10 x 6 m), so needs to be allowed space. It is hardy to zones 6–9.

Magnolia sieboldii (zones 6–9) has a wide growth habit (up to 40 ft/12 m across and 25 ft/8 m high). It has many attributes, not the least being that it flowers in early summer, so extending the magnolia flowering season. It has delightful, white, pendant flowers with (usually) bright crimson stamens, though there are those with either yellow or pink stamens. I have not seen these, but I cannot imagine that they are any more beautiful than the gorgeous scarlet. These flowers are also prettily scented. If you are able to plant M. *sieboldii* on a bank where there is a path beneath, you may have the pleasure of looking up into the nodding flowers.

You could not "have a soul above your boots" if you did not thrill to the sight of *Magnolia stellata* in full flower (see page 57). This species must surely be the best known of all magnolias, flowering as it does over several weeks, covering itself with starry flowers that have strap-like tepals and a pleasant, though not strong, perfume.

Magnolia stellata (zones 5–9) becomes a very twiggy sort of shrub if left unchecked and I think it makes good sense to remove a few lower branches, leaving a single stem and thus shaping it into a small tree (10 x 12 ft /3 x 4 m). Not only is this magnolia both pretty and dainty, its flowers are very frost hardy. A splendid hybrid from this species was raised at Boston's Arnold Arboretum in 1972 and named 'Centennial', as it was the arboretum's centennial year. This variety is notable for the large size of its flowers and some consider it the very best white *stellata*. Another raised in North America is 'Royal Star', and yet another is 'Waterlily'. From the gardener's point of view, all are perfectly acceptable, fitting into almost any garden and even able to enhance the modern courtyard if grown in suitably sized pots.

Because *Magnolia campbellii* is so spectacular it has been used in breeding. Some of the gorgeous results are lovely whites. *Magnolia* 'Sir Harold Hillier', its white flowers exceptionally beautiful, is befittingly named after a man closely associated with the history and development of the magnolia.

A comparatively recent introduction (1950) is the species *Magnolia cylindrica* (zones 6–9), with candle-like white flowers that have soft pink rays at the base. It does not concern us as gardeners that there has been botanical infighting over whether M. *cylindrica* is truly a species or a hybrid with M. *denudata*, because, be that as it may, as a plant M. *cylindrica* will provide you with beautiful flowers, and should not be overlooked. It is a small, spreading tree at 20 x 20 ft (6 x 6 m).

The superb *Magnolia denudata* (zones 6–9) is not only one of the most beautiful and beloved of magnolias, it is also the parent of some stunning hybrids, having had some very superior bedfellows. Following our white theme, I think my very favorite progeny is 'Snow White', which has not only such pretty flowers, but flowers that sit well on the branches, upright and poised. The flowers have more "form" than, say, M. *stellata*, while still forming a bushy shrub or small tree. I do not know exactly why I think it so special, but I look at it with particular pleasure each spring. It flowers for a long time, perhaps six weeks.

Pretty little 'Pristine', raised by Professor McDaniel of Illinois, has pure white flowers that are very refined and slim, sitting erect on the branches. It

Above: *Magnolia stellata* 'Royal Star'
Below: *Magnolia cylindrica*

Above: Professor McDaniel of Illinois raised 'Pristine', whose pure white flowers are very refined and slim.

grows into a graceful small tree of 18–20 ft (5.5–6 m).

We have discussed the remarkable hybrids bred by Dr. Todd Gresham (pages 47–49). Of course, some of them are white, and the following five appeal to me most, not only for their outstanding beauty, but because they are most vigorous and flower at an early age. From the Gresham stable I particularly favor 'David Clulow', with large cup-and-saucer flowers with a bit of pale pink at the base; 'Manchu Fan' has tulip-shaped flowers, again with a little pink at the base of the tepals; and 'Rouged Alabaster' is similar to the others and is another good white. I particularly like the splendid Gresham hybrid 'Sayonara', which has bowl-shaped, creamy flowers stained pink at the base, and 'Tina Durio', which has very large cup-and-saucer flowers which again are pink at the base. How I would hate to be without any of these magnolias.

Felix Jury of New Zealand aptly named his truly lovely white magnolia 'Lotus', for its flowers which are reminiscent of a water lily (see page 59). This tree is a true aristocrat, and, if you have can, plant it as a stand-alone specimen so its true beauty can be appreciated.

Magnolia 'Suishoren'

Something very different in white is 'Wada's Memory' (zones 6–8) from the well-known Japanese nursery of K. Sawada. This compact tree (28 x 20 ft/ 9 x 6 m) has droopy, floppy flowers, which do not sound so attractive but somehow are. It has a tremendous number of flowers, making a very lovely display. The new leaves are red, turning a deep green over the summer.

Before World War I, a German named Max Loebner crossed *Magnolia kobus* with M. *stellata*. The marriage has produced some of the most beautiful, accommodating and hardy small trees and shrubs. Some of these are blessedly white. *Magnolia* x *loebneri* 'Ballerina' (zones 5–9) is aptly named, for it is very dainty with many white flowers flushed pink when first open.

'Merrill' at 30 ft (10 m) is a bigger, more vigorous tree than 'Ballerina' at 15–20 ft (5–6 m) and has pure white flowers in the most tremendous profusion. It is another splendid specimen from the Arnold Arboretum. It flowers for a very long time, and seems impervious to the odd late frost.

'Spring Snow' was so named by Professor McDaniel of Illinois because in cold areas it sometimes flowers before spring snows have finished, but doesn't seem bothered by the cold (to zone 5). The flowers have a slight green tinge, which I always find very fetching.

All of the above *Magnolia* x *loebneri* are very desirable, be your garden large or small, and if your weather tends to be a bit awkward, these are the magnolias that can cope.

Magnolia 'Suishoren' is a little treasure. It has small, white flowers held very erect and grows into a small, shapely tree without any fuss. I do not know how it was bred, but because of its general appearance I think it has M. *denudata* in its ancestry.

While we talked about *Magnolia* x *soulangeana* in chapter 7, there are a few gorgeous white hybrids worthy of mention here. 'Lennei Alba' has very large, ivory-white flowers and is surely one of the best. M. 'Alba' (syn 'Alba Superba') is just that, and M. 'Brozzoni', with its nearly pure blooms with a hint of pink at the base, is thought by some to be the real aristocrat among all the soulangeanas.

Magnolia 'Lotus'

It is all very well to suggest so many white magnolias, but it is not likely that you can manage all thirty. Here are the ten I could not live without, my final selection of "to die for" white magnolias. As with all but the large-leafed species, these magnolias require a position in full sun to perform at their best.

Species or cultivar	Height x width	Hardiness zone
M. *campbellii* 'Strybing White'	50 x 30 ft (15 x 10 m)	7–9
M. *cylindrica*	20 x 20 ft (6 x 6 m)	6–9
M. *denudata*	30 x 30 ft (10 x 10 m)	6–9
M. 'Lotus'	30 x 12 ft (10 x 4 m)	6–9
M. 'Pristine'	20 x 6 ft (6 x 1.8 m)	6–9
M. 'Sayonara'	20 x 15 ft (6 x 5 m)	6–9
M. 'Snow White'	10 x 12 ft (3 x 4 m)	6–9
M. *stellata* 'Waterlily'	10 x 12 ft (3 x 4 m)	5–9
M. 'Suishoren'	20 x 6 ft (6 x 1.8 m)	6–9
M. 'Tina Durio'	20 x 15 ft (6 x 5 m)	6–9

CHAPTER 9

To Die For

The Best in Pink

Pink is such a feminine color that it tends to conjure up pictures of small and dainty. Not so for some of the most beautiful of the magnolias. In talking of the very best in pink, we have to start with the noble species *campbellii* and its subspecies *mollicomata*. Not everyone has room to grow something that will, in time, grow so very large (up to 100 ft/30 m) and that is also prone to damage from frosts (zones 7–9), flowering at the end of winter. Certainly in my own garden, only about once in every three years do I see the full glory of its flowering, but all I can say is, it's still worth it. The display of pink cup-and-saucer flowers is magnificent, a quite unforgettable sight. While you have to wait for its first flowering, if you plant either *campbellii* or *mollicomata* with magnolias that flower at a younger age, you will not be flowerless while waiting. It is very important that you do not buy seedling *Magnolia campbellii*, as they take an extremely long time to flower (20 years) and could also have variable color. Grafted plants will flower in half the time, but this can still take ten years.

The eastern form of *Magnolia campbellii* subsp *mollicomata* flowers later in the season and at a younger age (six years) and, what's more, it has even more flowers, so it is highly recommended. A marriage of M. *campbellii* with M. *campbellii* subsp *mollicomata* produced the incomparable 'Charles Raffill', which blooms later, an advantage in colder cli-

Opposite: For beauty of flower, and for elegant presentation, it would be difficult to find any better than the sumptuous *campbelli* 'Charles Raffill'.

mates. It is a deeper pink than *campbellii* or *mollicomata*. In fact, these magnolias are very much alike, so you could not go wrong in choosing any or all, for they are among the aristocrats of the magnolia world. Indeed, there are perhaps few species of tree more beautiful in flower than M. *campbellii* and its close relatives.

Magnolia dawsoniana (zones 7–9) has floppy pink flowers that are much more attractive than its description leads you to believe. The general effect of this profusely blooming tree is quite spectacular, it is just that the individual blooms don't have great form. Clarke Nursery in California produced another beautiful form of *dawsoniana*, not surprisingly called 'Clarke'. I have not yet seen it, but it is very highly regarded for its rich pink color and its hardiness. The British expert Graham Rankin thinks that 'Clarke' cannot be matched by any other *dawsoniana* cultivar, and, as a leading magnolia authority and author of *Magnolia: A Hamlyn Care Manual*, he is certainly very well qualified to judge.

When it comes to *Magnolia sargentiana*, the best pink is M. *sargentiana* var *robusta*. As its name suggests, it is more robust. *Magnolia sargentiana* abhors wind, but is otherwise hardy to zone 7. The flowers of *robusta* are a beautiful rose-pink that darkens at the base; in full flower the tree is a magnificent sight. A cultivar from the Strybing Arboretum in San Francisco, called 'Blood Moon', is darker in color and hardier (zone 5). I think it sounds wonderful, but sadly I have not yet seen it.

Magnolia sprengeri is beautiful in itself, but there is a particularly stunning form called 'Diva', with

Above left: 'Star Wars' has flowers of a strange spiky shape.
Above right: 'Caerhay's' Belle'

fragrant pink flowers in most generous numbers. It is not only desirable for its beauty, but it is also quite hardy (zone 5).

The last species with pink flowers that I shall mention is *Magnolia stellata*, very probably one of the most popular magnolias (hardy to zones 5–9). The form *rosea* is pink, but like 'King Rose', it fades to white. One of the most beautiful *stellata* is from Portland, Oregon, and is named 'Jane Platt' after the owner of the garden in which it was discovered. With its rich, deep pink flowers and extremely floriferous habit, it is not to be overlooked.

While Felix Jury's hybrid output was small compared with Dr. Todd Gresham's, it was also very select. There are certainly some outstanding pinks among the Jury hybrids, of which 'Athene' has to be one of the most striking, mainly because, not only are its flowers very beautiful, but there are so many of them. They are actually pink and white, but the overall effect is pink. 'Atlas' has huge flowers of an appealing, fresh pink. If you like gigantic flowers, this magnolia is for you, but remember to give it

some shelter because, although it is somewhat hardy (zones 6–9), the large flowers invite the wind to tear them.

Magnolia 'Milky Way' was bred the same way as 'Athene', so that it is both pink and white, but pink dominates. The flowers sit very neatly along the branches, and they are scented. 'Mark Jury', though not actually bred but only named by Felix Jury, is a wonderfully scented cup-and-saucer flower in a soft shade of lilac pink.

The last pink Jury hybrid I shall mention is probably the most popular and highly regarded worldwide. This is 'Iolanthe', whose absolutely enormous buds do not belie their promise, for the pink-tinged-lavender flowers are both large and very handsome. It is an arresting sight as a mature tree in full bloom and has few faults.

Two other hybrids that are both pink and desirable were bred by Oswald Blumhardt of Whangarei, New Zealand. 'Star Wars' has flowers of a strange, spiky shape in bright pink, with its most favored attribute being that it flowers for many weeks, and then may do so intermittently until the fall. This late blooming does not seem to diminish the number of flowers in the spring. 'Early Rose' is a

Above: The buds of 'Sweetheart'.
Left: 'Athene'

sister seedling with much the same virtues and, as its name implies, it flowers early enough in the season to occasionally catch a late frost, which will damage the flowers.

The alliance between *Magnolia sargentiana* var *robusta* and M. *sprengeri* 'Diva' produced at least three wonderful pinks. The first to flower is 'Caerhay's Belle' (zones 6–9), which is salmon-pink with a velvet look to its tepals. It is magnificent, despite the fact that its flowers lack good form, but they make up for this by being big and blowsy and the tree simply smothered—an exciting sight early in the spring.

'Susanna van Veen' (zones 6–9) is a darker purple and its flowers do not even have a passing acquaintance with form, but, having said that, I consider that, like any magnolia, it is full of charm and what's wrong with being different?

The third offering is called 'Sweetheart' (zones 6–9). It is a grandchild of the royal marriage of *Magnolia sargentiana* var *robusta* and M. *sprengeri* 'Diva'. A seedling from 'Caerhay's Belle' and raised by

Magnolia × *loebneri* 'Leonard Messel' is beautiful in pink, generous, hardy to zones 5–9 and very long-flowering.

Peter Cave of Hamilton, New Zealand, it is just lovely, a very beautiful pink and flowers later than 'Caerhay's Belle', an advantage if there are frosts around.

Dr. Todd Gresham's name has appeared often in this book, but that is because he was such an important figure in the world of magnolias, being responsible for breeding some of the most beautiful and garden-worthy hybrids. Of course, among all of his hybrids there are some very special pinks. One of the early Gresham introductions was 'Heaven Scent' (zones 6–9). Although scent seems to be singularly lacking, as mentioned earlier, the pink flower with a hint of lavender is very pretty and there are plenty of them, for when the tree is in full bloom you can scarcely see a branch. Its growth habit is broad (20 ft/6 m), so give it some lateral space, though as a tree it would be just classed as small.

'Peppermint Stick' (zones 6–9), which is actually white with pink stripes, gives the general appearance of pink when the flowers are full out. However, while the flowers at that stage are just pleasantly garden-worthy the buds are superb. They sit along the branches with great poise, tall and slim. I think that they have the prettiest buds of any hybrid.

There is also the splendid magnolia named after Dr. Gresham, aptly called 'Todd Gresham' (zones 6–9), with cup-shaped flowers in a rich pink. It surely shows the quality that allowed it to be named after its breeder.

Different altogether is one of my all-time favorites, *Magnolia* x *loebneri* 'Leonard Messel'. Its pink, star-like flowers are glorious. Of course, it is very hardy (zone 5) for a magnolia, laughs at frost and flowers for an extended time. It also has good fall color. Naturally, I find all this very acceptable, but I grow it primarily for its sheer beauty of flower. It is difficult to describe, but it would rival any flowering tree. And because of its small size, it will fit into most any garden, so I strongly commend it.

'Pinkie' is my favorite of the American "Little Girls" (a group of small-growing magnolias bred at the U.S. National Arboretum in Washington D.C., see page 12). It has pleasant pink flowers that are bigger than those of its sisters. It seems to flower for a long time, and grows into quite a stout lady. As 'Pinkie' flowers quite late in the season, it provides fresh flowers when others are fading.

The *soulangeana* hybrids are discussed in chapter 7, so I shall just mention two favorites in pink. The first is 'San Jose', introduced by Clarke Nursery of California. Apparently, there is some confusion, for the plant widely grown in Britain and New Zealand is not the same as the definitive North American. Clarke's version is dark pink, where the British and New Zealand ones are predominantly pink overlaying a white base. Either 'San Jose' is very acceptable.

Today, *Magnolia* x *soulangeana* 'Alexandrina' (zones 5–9) would probably fall into the old-fashioned category (i.e., it is not a modern hybrid), but it can still hold its own. Developed in 1831, its flowers are strong pink at the base, fading to white near the top. There are various clones bearing the same name, as things have got a bit muddled over the year; however, if it is a *soulangeana* it will be acceptable, even if its name is a bit suspect.

'Verbanica' (zones 5–9) is a lovely clear pink, flowering later than its siblings and 'Daybreak' (zones 5–9) is a newer American hybrid bred by Dr. August Kehr. It has scented, rose pink flowers.

I waited many years to acquire the splendid 'Princess Margaret' (zones 7–9), which is well named for it is certainly blue-blooded, having *Magnolia campbellii* and M. *sargentiana* for parents. It has deep pink flowers of a cup-and-saucer shape, and was first called 'Windsor Belle', for it was raised at Windsor, England. When it was discovered how splendid the flowers are it was renamed 'Princess Margaret'. You must wait a year or two for it to flower, but the wait is well worthwhile.

Of the thirty pinks I think so very desirable, I consider these ten the very best, not only for beauty, but for more mundane reasons like hardiness and size. All of these magnolias like full sun.

Species or cultivar	Height x width	Hardiness zone
M. 'Athene'	30 x 15 ft (10 x 5 m)	6–9
M. *campbellii* 'Charles Raffill'	50 x 30 ft (15 x 10 m)	7–9
M. *campbellii* subsp *mollicomata*	50 x 30 ft (15 x 10 m)	7–9
M. *dawsoniana*	50 x 30 ft (15 x 10 m)	7–9
M. x *loebneri* 'Leonard Messel'	25 x 20 ft (8 x 6 m)	5–9
M. 'Mark Jury'	50 x 15 ft (15 x 5 m)	7–9
M. 'Peppermint Stick'	30 x 20 ft (10 x 6 m)	6–9
M. 'Princess Margaret'	50 x 30 ft (15 x 10 m)	7–9
M. *sprengeri* 'Diva'	50 x 30 ft (15 x 10 m)	5–9
M. 'Sweetheart'	50 x 30 ft (15 x 10 m)	6–9

CHAPTER 10

To Die For

The Best in Red and Purple

The descriptions of colors, here, red or purple, will be what you might rightfully call "loose", as they were in the other chapters on color, but they do serve to indicate the color range into which these magnolias fall. For these rich colors, which have royal connotations, the first to be mentioned would have to be that wonderful form of *Magnolia campbellii* known as 'Darjeeling' (zones 7–9), with dark purple-crimson flowers and the usual wonderful poise of its species. An offspring of 'Darjeeling' called 'Betty Jessel' is just as gorgeous. It is the latest of the *campbelliis* to flower, which is a real plus, because, as has often been mentioned, early-flowering magnolias can be sometimes frosted if you are in that sort of climate.

Magnolia 'Mary Williams' has rose-purple flowers and is a clone of M. *campbellii* subsp *mollicomata*, as is the incomparable 'Lanarth' (both zones 7–9), whose color is so stunning that it has been used extensively in breeding programs. Should you be so unfortunate as to have to choose just one magnolia, I think you could be very tempted to choose 'Lanarth', for its color is quite incredible, it is very vigorous and it has wonderfully large, woolly buds.

Magnolia dawsoniana has a stunning red form called 'Chyverton Red' (zones 7–9). When its flowers first open, they are an astonishing crimson, somehow a color you perhaps do not associate with (at least the more ordinary range of) magnolias. This makes it special, even before considering that

Opposite: One of the "Little Girls", 'Ann' is a very attractive purple and a particularly good magnolia for small gardens.

Above: When *Magnolia dawsoniana* 'Chyverton Red' first opens the flowers are an astonishing crimson color. The flowers are also tolerant of light frost and appear over a long period of time.

it is particularly frost tolerant and flowers for many weeks.

Magnolia liliiflora is sometimes called the woody orchid, for the flowers look like orchids. But not, I must say, to me. Be that as it may, it is a bushy shrub and two of its forms are the most wonderful color. 'Nigra' is most deservedly popular, with flowers of a very rich, dark purple (zones 6–9). Then there is the American introduction 'O'Neill' (zones 6–9), which is an even darker purple with larger flowers. These plants flower over a very long period (six weeks) and could look very well planted with some yellow varieties, which also tend to flower later in the season.

The lovely *Magnolia sprengeri* 'Diva' (zones 7–9) has produced some choice seedlings of which 'Burncoose' is a gorgeous pinkish purple. Its upright habit of growth makes it ideal for smaller spaces.

I am very fond of a magnolia called 'Caerhay's Surprise' (zones 6–9). Although the original flower color does fade (which is true of many taxa), the red-purple flowers are most spectacular, especially as they have a spiky look. This obliging magnolia flowers for many weeks, its delightful habit probably inherited from its *liliiflora* blood.

Some of the famous American "Little Girls" have lovely dark colors (see page 12). 'Ann' (zones 3–9), 'Betty', 'Judy', 'Ricki', and 'Susan' are all dark (zones 5–9), and perhaps a little too like each other, but they certainly share a most acceptable deep purple color. They are particularly useful in small

Above left: 'Caerhay's Surprise'
Above right: *Magnolia liliiflora* 'Nigra' is most deservedly popular for its wonderful dark color.

gardens, (growing to just 12 ft/3 m). I have not actually seen Todd Gresham's 'Deep Purple Dream', but from photographs its goblet-shaped flowers look to be the most amazing dark color (zones 6–9). From the same breeder comes 'Royal Crown' (zones 6–9) with dark red-purple flowers that are white within. It is not particularly special, but it flowers early and for a long time, the color is good and if you use your imagination a little, the shape is reminiscent of a crown.

Now we come to Felix Jury's 'Apollo' (zones 6–9). This is truly a class act, with star-shaped flowers in a lovely violet purple, and there are so many

Above left: 'Black Tulip'
Above right: 'Philip Tregunna'

of them. The tepals have a heavy texture and the blooms are strongly scented. I would give 'Apollo' ten out of ten without hesitation. Perhaps 'Vulcan' (zones 6–9) would not score quite so highly, because it, like some prima donnas, shows quite a lot of temperament, just like the little girl of nursery rhyme fame "when it is good it is very very good, and when its is bad it is horrid". For its best, you have to have a little patience, because when the young tree flowers, the flowers are juvenile and the color a rather murky pink. But wait a year or two and there is a metamorphosis. The flowers are then a wonderful ruby color, and the size quite large. 'Vulcan' in full mature flower is an arresting sight.

Mark Jury has released a magnolia he has called 'Black Tulip' (zones 6–9). The color is wonderfully dark, a deep true purple. As yet, I find the flower a bit stubby, but that may improve with time. It would be difficult to improve upon the color.

Magnolia 'Felix Jury' (zones 6–9) is named after its breeder, so you would expect it to be special, and it is. The color is neither red nor wine, but somewhere in between, and the flowers truly quite enormous (15 in/38 cm). Usually, I would be inclined to turn away from something so large, but instead I find myself filled with admiration at its magnificence. I think that M. 'Felix Jury' will become internationally admired, which is a very fitting way of honoring a most important magnolia hybridizer.

I nearly forgot to mention a choice Gresham hybrid called 'Joe McDaniel'. Its bowl-shaped

Magnolia 'Spectrum'

flowers are a very deep pleasing purple, with a striking contrast in that the inner sides of the tepals are white. Like all the Gresham hybrids, it flowers from a young age (two years), is hardy to zone 6 and generally trouble-free.

Magnolia 'Galaxy' and 'Spectrum' (zones 5–9), from Dr. Kehr of the U.S. National Arboretum, are both purple-colored, 'Galaxy' being a darker color than 'Spectrum'. These are sister seedlings and I feel you would not really need both, unless you have lots of room.

Then we come to the ever-so-reliable soulangeanas, all hardy to zone 5. 'Burgundy', from Clarke Nursery of San Jose, is a lovely dark color. The wonderful 'Lennei' has color so good—a very deep purple—it has been used extensively in breeding. The insides of the tepals are white, which is a very fetching combination. *Magnolia* 'Rustica Rubra' is similar, but without the same charisma; however, like the others of this breeding, it is absolutely reliable.

Magnolia 'Picture' (zone 5–9) is rather different from its relations. It was introduced by the Japanese firm, Wadas Nursery, and has tall flowers of purple on the outside, paler inside. The upright poise of the blooms is most attractive and the flowers are very large for a *soulangeana*. Mr Amos Pickard of Kent, England, raised some seedlings of 'Picture' of which 'Pickard's Ruby' (zones 5–9) is a very good, dark color.

My very favorite red and purple magnolias, listed here, have been chosen for their spectacular color and shape. They are at their best in full sun.

Species or cultivar	Height x width	Hardiness zone
M. 'Apollo'	40 x 20 ft (12 x 6 m)	6–9
M. *campbellii* 'Betty Jessel'	50 x 30 ft (15 x 10 m)	7–9
M. *sprengeri* 'Burncoose Purple'	50 x 30 ft (15 x 10 m)	5–9
M. 'Caerhay's Surprise'	50 x 30 ft (15 x 10 m)	6–9
M. *campbellii* 'Darjeeling'	50 x 30 ft (15 x 10 m)	7–9
M. *campbellii* subsp *mollicomata* 'Lanarth'	50 x 30 ft (15 x 10 m)	7–9
M. *dawsoniana* 'Chyverton Red'	50 x 30 ft (15 x 10 m)	7–9
M. 'Felix Jury'	30 x 12 ft (10 x 3.5 m)	6–9
M. *liliiflora* 'Nigra'	10 x 8 ft (3 x 2.5 m)	6–9
M. 'Vulcan'	30 x 10 ft (10 x 3 m)	6–9

CHAPTER 11

To Die For

The Best in Yellow, and Some Others

Magnolia acuminata is a very important tree from eastern North America. Not so for the tree itself, handsome as it is, nor for its very small, insignificant flower, obscurely nestled in leaves, but rather for the yellow color of its flowers. Many of us had not seen yellow magnolias until comparatively recent years, but how astonished and delighted we were when these become available. And they have become so because hybridists, particularly from the Brooklyn Botanic Garden, could see the potential for breeding not only for the color of *acuminata*, but also for its great hardiness (zone 4).

Perhaps you would not grow this species itself, but certainly you might consider the selected forms 'Golden Glow' and 'Koban Dori' if you had lots of room, just for interest. But very probably it would be infinitely more rewarding to grow the hybrids.

For over forty years, the Brooklyn Botanic Garden team, initially under the direction of Dr. Eva Maria Sperber, worked on crossing *Magnolia acuminata* with the Asiatic species M. *denudata* and M. *liliiflora*. This was the first time such a mixed marriage had taken place, and a highly successful union it turned out to be.

The *Magnolia denudata* cross produced the lovely 'Elizabeth' (zones 6–9), which has glorious, primrose-yellow, scented, goblet-shaped flowers. It is just

Above: 'Elizabeth', bred at the Brooklyn Botanic Gardens, has glorious, scented, primrose-yellow flowers.

Above: 'Yellow Fever' has shimmering pale yellow flowers.
Right: *Magnolia* × *brooklynensis* 'Woodsman'

lovely, a real treasure, flowering late enough to escape those unwelcome late frosts. The same breeding produced 'Sundance' (zones 6–9), which is well named, for its pale yellow flowers appear to dance along the branches. 'Butterflies' (zones 5–9) is a more recent introduction from this same breeding by Phil Savage of Michigan. Described as light yellow with red stamens, it has not yet flowered in my garden, but magnolia expert Dorothy Callaway, who wrote *The World of Magnolias*, expects 'Butterflies' to become one of the most popular magnolia hybrids. I do not know if she was restricting this to yellow-flowered magnolias only or the whole range, but it makes waiting for my first flowering very exciting.

That is the thing about magnolias, they are truly exciting, and you always seem to be waiting for a new one to flower. By this, I do not necessarily mean a new variety, just those in your garden that have yet to flower. Anticipation adds a real spice to

gardening! This is certainly the case with my latest, yet-to-flower yellow magnolia, called 'Sun Ray' (zones 6–9). Another lovely, scented, prolific primrose-yellow magnolia is 'Yellow Fever' (zones 6–9). Rumor has it that Mr. Savage's 'Gold Star' (zones 5–9) is really something, because it is a soft yellow *Magnolia stellata*, which you can imagine will be a great addition to any collection, and ideal in the small garden. 'Yellow Bird' (zones 6–9) is a wonderful color, quite a bright, pure yellow, but spoiled in that the leaves come out at the same time as the flowers, so although you can see the first few flowers, after that they are hidden. But, on balance, I think it worth growing just for that first week or so when the "birds" show up so well.

Then there are what I call "designer" colors, very difficult to describe and very different from other magnolia colors. Again developed by the Brooklyn Botanic Garden team, from a cross between *Magnolia acuminata* and M. *liliiflora*, the first I saw flower was 'Woodsman' (zones 5–9). I was astonished; the flowers are purple in bud, and when open they are a sort of chartreuse-green tinged with yellow and purple. It might sound unattractive, but not so, for the flower is very attractive, the sort that grows on you. In a garden, the tree, although large (35 ft/10 m) does not make a shouting statement and the leaves come before the flowers have finished, which is a bit of a minus. Nevertheless, I certainly would not be without 'Woodsman', and if I were a floral artist, I would probably not be able to believe my luck to have such colors to work with.

From the same cross comes 'Eva Maria' (zones 5–9), named after Dr. Eva Maria Sperber. Again, there is some difficulty providing an adequate description, but the tulip-shaped flowers are a sort of magenta pink with dashes of yellow and green. It might not sound great, but it is actually very pretty and intriguingly different. There are quite a number

'Yellow Bird'

of varieties from this cross, and what are called back crosses, but I have not yet seen them. So as I mentioned above, there is that exciting thing called anticipation.

My favorites are not difficult to choose here because the list is so much shorter. Yellow is still a new development in magnolias. These magnolias like a site in full sun and have the same cultivation requirements as outlined in Chapter 2 (page 17).	Species or cultivar	Height x width	Hardiness zone
	M. 'Elizabeth'	30 x 20 ft (10 x 6 m)	6–9
	M. 'Eva Maria'	30 x 20 ft (10 x 6 m)	5–9
	M. 'Sundance'	30 x 20 ft (10 x 6 m)	6–9
	M. 'Woodsman'	30 x 20 ft (10 x 6 m)	5–9
	M. 'Yellow Fever'	30 x 20 ft (10 x 6 m)	6–9

CHAPTER 12

The Magnificent Magnolia

North American Grandeur

For me, *Magnolia grandiflora* immediately conjures visions of the American South, of colonnaded mansions surrounded by these stately trees. Perfume wafts through the warm air and lovely ladies with parasols stroll through the gardens. Very "Gone with the Wind"ish. However, this wonderful tree is very much more than a prop for a romantic film.

Magnolia grandiflora (also known as the bull bay and southern magnolia) is native to the southern United States and ranges from eastern North Carolina, along the Atlantic Coast to central Florida. It then ranges west from southern Georgia, Alabama and Mississippi, through Louisiana and into southeast Texas. *Magnolia grandiflora* prefers to be never too far from the Atlantic Ocean or the Gulf of Mexico, for, hardy to only zones 7–8, it does not like to be too chilly. Temperatures below -9°C (15°F) or above 38°C (100°F) occur only rarely through this species' natural range.

The words to describe it will always include "majestic" and "grand," because that is how it is—very tall (115 ft/135 m), with enormous, shiny, leathery leaves that have pleasing tan indumentum underneath, and stunning, scented flowers in huge lovely bowls.

This generous evergreen tree flowers all through the summer months, not a spectacular display all at

once like the deciduous magnolias, but more restrained. Each flower lasts two days, but if you wish to have a flower on your dinner table, you had better plan to eat at midday. I well remember setting the dinner table for guests, adding a floating bowl of a lovely magnolia, and then in late evening ushering the guests to the table to find it had literally shut up shop, not to open again until morning.

It is surprising, then, to learn that a magnolia from the warm South can flourish in unkind climates. Mind you, it is very often planted against a wall and so protected from some cold and frost. It is like anything else—if you really want something, you will go to extraordinary lengths to achieve your aim. Choosing the warmest site in what are alien

Opposite: The magnificent flowers of *Magnolia grandiflora* last only a couple of days, but they keep appearing over many months.
Above right: The delectable buds of *Magnolia grandiflora* 'St Mary' are nearly as beautiful as the flowers.

climes, and using heavy mulch to prevent deep-seated frost are methods that have been successful in colder zones (6–7), but it is trial and error, as it is with any plant outside its natural habitat. How fortunate are those of us who live in temperate or subtropical areas and who can therefore grow *Magnolia grandiflora* at will.

The phase "grow at will" should perhaps be qualified, for you surely need space for this stately tree. There is, however, a variety called 'Little Gem'. Gem I am sure it is, little I am sure it is not. Not unless you think 20 ft (6 m) is small. But, compared to the larger varieties that reach 60 feet high and 40 feet wide (18 x 12 m), I guess it is! However, it is necessary to be practical, or reasonably so. Many gardens, even if not very large, can manage and should have one focal tree. If you wish to screen an unattractive view, *Magnolia grandiflora* would be just the thing, as you need an evergreen for this purpose. If you wished for shade, what could be better than *grandiflora*? Of course, if you have a large garden or perhaps the blessing of a field, how much pleasure you would give yourself by planting—very widely spaced—more than one M. *grandiflora*.

The quality of *Magnolia grandiflora* grown from seed can be highly variable and with modern methods of propagation different varieties are readily available. I find it fascinating to read in J. M. (Jim) Gardiner's definitive and splendid book, *Magnolias: A Gardener's Guide*, that, in the 19th century, scaffolding with platforms at various levels was built around the tree so that branches could be air-layered and then sold for big money. This practice quite often killed the mother tree, but I suppose by that time there were plenty of its healthy "children" about.

There are a good number of named selections available, all with the creamy white flowers of the species, and it is advisable to purchase these as they will flower when very young, as against seedlings that can take many years. 'Edith Bogue' is the one to choose for (relatively) cooler climates, for it is

hardy to zone 7 (the other hybrids being happier in zone 8 or warmer). After that, I think that other than the previously discussed 'Little Gem' you may choose large or larger with or without the attractive russet indumentum.

Magnolia grandiflora 'Exmouth' comes into the tried-and-true category, for it has been propagated for more than a century. It is taller and slimmer than some and produces many flowers. Then there are varieties called 'Ferruginea' (noted for its wonderful indumentum) and 'Goliath', whose flowers are huge (8–12 in/20–30 cm) but which doesn't have much indumentum. 'Russet' has lots of indumentum and a compact habit; 'Samuel Sommer' has the very best leaves, very deep green and polished looking, and simply huge flowers (14 in/35 cm). 'St. Mary' is a little smaller growing, which at 20–26 ft (6–8 m) still doesn't exactly make it a dwarf.

A particularly attractive *Magnolia grandiflora* is 'Bracken's Brown Beauty', because it has a neat, pyramidal shape, very nice brown indumentum and smaller (5–6 in/13–15 cm) but still very desirable fragrant flowers. 'Charles Dickens', another selection, has nothing to do with the British novelist. Rather it was named after a Tennessee gentleman in whose garden it was found. It is distinguished by huge flowers (over 12 in/30 cm) and bright red fruits. 'Claudia Wannamaker' offers a different benefit, for though its flowers are small (3$\frac{1}{4}$ in/8 cm) it flowers continuously over five months. 'Majestic Beauty' is well named, for it is very large, 60 feet high by 20 feet wide (18 x 6 m) with bright flowers in profusion over a three-month period.

Magnolia grandiflora is obviously very highly regarded to have had so much work done on the one species. I do not think that anyone would deny its splendor, for it is like no other evergreen tree, offering magnificence in size and presence, beauty of leaf and unparalleled flowers of creamy white, exuding the most sensuous lemon scent. Besides all the virtues listed, I have failed to mention an attribute that I find very unusual in a tree with such enor-

Above: Suited to the large garden, *Magnolia grandiflora* 'Goliath' is a majestic tree.
Left: The seed heads of *Magnolia grandiflora* 'Majestic Beauty' give a beautiful extra dimension to this cultivar.

mous leaves—it is very wind tolerant, though it must also be sheltered from desiccating winds.

Many people in the South consider it the *only* magnolia, and I freely and happily admit that no magnolia garden worthy of the name should be without selections of *Magnolia grandiflora*. Indeed, it is regarded so highly that it is the state flower of Mississippi and Louisiana, and during the American Civil War it was the emblem of the Confederacy. So, while the Southerners have first claim, the rest of the world appreciates this splendid magnolia and regards it with both pleasure and awe. I do sincerely recommend it to you if you are fortunate enough to have both the space and the climate to suit this treasure.

CHAPTER 13

For Something Different

The Rare and the Special

Somehow, if anything is described as rare you immediately lust to own it. Some species magnolia come into this category, but most are not of interest to the general gardener. Also, from a gardener's point of view there is not space for everything. Having said that, though, it is fun to have one or two that are perhaps not all that rare, but which are certainly unusual. Into this category comes the American native species *Magnolia macrophylla*. It has the most colossal leaves—they can be as long as 3 ft (70 cm). The texture is rather thin and papery, which you would perhaps not expect in a magnolia, but the light shines prettily through them. It is not known as the umbrella tree for nothing, for the leaves are arranged like an umbrella and shelter the enormous, scented flowers of cream, tinted purple at the base.

Because its leaves are so enormous, it is necessary to provide this tree with lots of room and good shelter. In its native habitat, it grows in sheltered valleys or on the lower slopes of hills. For all its size (40–50 ft/12–15 m), it is not a clumsy tree, and although it has a tropical look about it, it is actually hardy to zone 6.

The flowers are, of course, more than acceptable, but do tend to get overlooked because when they appear in mid-summer they are somewhat hidden by the large leaves. Also, to prevent wind damage the tree is often planted down a bank where the flowers are not so obvious.

Opposite: *Magnolia amoena* is a little tree from China with white flowers that are heavily flushed reddish-pink.

Above: *Magnolia macrophylla* subsp *ashei* has enormous tropical-looking leaves with attractive flowers.

Some forms have been selected; Phil Savage has bred hybrids between *Magnolia macrophylla* and *M. virginiana* that are said to be very fine. Two that have been named are 'Karl Flink' and 'Brigitta Flink'.

Magnolia macrophylla subsp *ashei* (syn *M. ashei*) really is rare (and very difficult to source), so I look at it in our garden with some awe. A native of northwest Florida it enjoys warmer climates (zones 7–9) and reaches anywhere between 30 and 70 ft (10–20 m). It seems quite happy and differs only in the smaller size of the leaves and flowers from

While the flowers of *Magnolia delavayi* can be hard to see, the tree itself is spectacular.

M. macrophylla. It is different, but also beautiful and fun to grow.

Magnolia tripetala grows to 40 ft (12 m) and to my eye does not seem so very different, except that the flowers smell far from agreeable, but they look very good. You can best admire them from a little distance, especially in their earlier stages when they have a candle-like stance. Planted in a woodland situation, which is what this native North American species likes, it not only provides light shade, but also an exotic, tropical look. It will grow in zones 4–9.

Very recently, I saw a truly beautiful species magnolia, and more recently I was fortunate enough to acquire it. *Magnolia amoena,* which translates to "beautiful magnolia". And so it is. A little tree from China (zones 7–11; 12 ft/3.5 m), the version I saw was white with bold reddish pink stripes, although books call it pink, and I liked it very much. I have had mine for two years and it has not yet bloomed.

What would happen if you had a large space in your garden awaiting a treasure? Well, you could plant what is considered one of the most spectacular of evergreen trees. *Magnolia delavayi* hails from just one place, Yunnan province in China. It is a grand tree with enormous leaves, up to 15 in (37 cm) long and 8 in (20 cm) wide, which are its chief beauty. The tree is multi-stemmed, which means that, while it grows tall, it also grows very wide (30 x 30 ft/10 x 10 m). It looks tropical but is surpris-

ingly hardy to zones 7–8. The flowers are not a plus; the great magnolia authority G. K. Johnstone described them as "sadly fugitive." This is indeed so, for they appear best at night, which is very inconvenient, and last up to about three days, but often less. But then again the flowers of the splendid and universally acclaimed *M. grandiflora* last only two. I sometimes think that if the flower is fleeting it concentrates your considered attention wonderfully, for if you know time is limited, you study the beauty carefully. For *M. delavayi* is a beautiful flower. I think the fat, pale green buds, then the globe shape of the flowers before they fully open, are most delectable; at this stage the flowers are lemon green. Then they open wide, turn ivory white in color and are most beautifully scented. The writers who have expressed disappointment in the flowers are men. Maybe they like something more flamboyant, which certainly you could rightfully expect from the appearance of the tree, but I find a subtle beauty in the flowers and the buds are delicious. The blooms come intermittently over a two- or three-month period, so there is never a spectacular display.

Having said all this, why grow *Magnolia delavayi*? Because it is so very handsome, quite well worth growing for the huge leaves alone, which are a pleasing matt green rather than shiny, and very clean looking, especially underneath because they do not have indumentum. Then it grows to a noble size, both upward and outward. The buds are gorgeous, the flowers deliciously scented, the color attractive. Lastly, not many gardeners, perhaps because of restriction of space, or simply not knowing about it, grow *M. delavayi*, so you could have a special treasure, all the while helping to preserve a splendid tree.

Trees like these would add a good deal of interest to your garden, if you have plenty of space. If not, and you had to choose, it is doubtful they would provide you with quite the pleasure and beauty as do the superb (and smaller) Asiatic magnolias.

An Extra Dimension

Perfume

It may sound greedy, but it is excellent to grow a plant that can offer more than just one attribute. In other words, you probably choose magnolias for their beautiful flowers, but many offer sweet perfume as well. Of course, you will still choose for beauty of flower as a priority, but where two magnolias seem equally beautiful and suitable to you, if one is also perfumed it adds an extra and very desirable dimension.

For small gardens, obviously smaller magnolias are the most suitable, and the most suitable of all is the species M. *stellata* and its cultivars (zones 5–9), most of which are scented. If we are to choose just two of these, I think 'Waterlily' and 'Centennial' would be very acceptable. For a lovely, scented, small magnolia in a dark color I suggest 'Ann' (zones 3–9), one of the "Little Girls." Its color is also especially good as many of the scented magnolias are either white or close to white.

Any small garden could be beautifully enhanced by my very favorite *Magnolia* x *loebneri* 'Leonard Messel' (zones 5–9), which has star-like flowers in soft lilac pink that are delightfully scented. Other forms of this lovely subject that are also scented are

Above: For any garden *Magnolia stellata* is ideal, but it is particularly suited to the small garden, where its perfume can be appreciated.

Above: 'Serene' is dark purple and sensuously perfumed.
Right: 'Daybreak'

called 'Pristine' (zones 6–9), with a smaller, rather dainty, scented flower, and then another of my very favorites, 'Snow White' (zones 6–9), with neat white flowers sitting upright on the branches. In fact, 'Snow White' would fit most admirably into the small garden.

At least five (and probably more) of Felix Jury's stunning hybrids are beautifully scented but I do not think you could plant anything more pleasing for both beauty of flower and pleasing perfume than 'Athene', 'Milky Way', 'Apollo', 'Serene' or the incomparable 'Vulcan' (all zones 6–9). As has been mentioned, scented magnolias are often pale in color, and indeed 'Athene' and 'Milky Way' are, but you would have a beautiful contrast should you plant the gorgeous, dark violet-colored 'Apollo' or the stunning red-purple 'Vulcan'.

Todd Gresham bred wonderful magnolias and, of course, some are scented. My choices would be

'Ballerina' and 'Merrill' (zones 5–9). As has been mentioned in the cultivation section, for small gardens it is advisable to prune to a single stem, both to aid underplanting and to conserve space.

To extend the flowering season, the species *Magnolia sieboldii* (zones 6–9) is splendid. Its nodding flowers with scarlet bosses of stamens are lemon scented, and although the leaves are out before the flowers, this does not seem to matter, as the pleasant green leaves frame the downward-facing flowers. In fact, M. *sieboldii* is a choice subject for any garden, large or small.

For the medium-sized garden any of the above are suitable, but you can include the following larger magnolias. First to come to mind is a magnolia of incomparable pristine beauty and sweet fragrance, and beloved by many, the species M. *denudata*. Bred from this beauty is one actually

Above: *Magnolia × loebneri* 'Leonard Messel'

'Manchu Fan', 'Tina Durio', 'Sayonara' and 'Rouged Alabaster' (zones 6–9), for even if they were not perfumed, they are still some of my very favorite magnolias. These all have white or cream flowers with a flush of pink.

The sweetly scented 'Wada's Memory' (zones 6–8) would not be to everybody's taste because the flowers flop down in an exhausted-looking way, so you wouldn't grow them for their form. But forget that, do not try to use them for floral art, and instead stand back and look at the tree in full flower. I think you would change your mind, for it is a shimmering pillar of white.

For the large garden, grow any of the scented magnolias already mentioned plus some additional, very large, but very choice subjects. You could not possibly overlook the wonderful native American species *Magnolia grandiflora* (zones 7–9), which besides its enormous size, wonderful shining leaves and elegant flowers, has the most beautiful, sensuous, lemon scent. You could appropriately grow a cultivar called 'Goliath', though I must say that all *grandiflora* of my acquaintance have grown large, and that includes the variety called 'Little Gem'. M. *grandiflora* is a special tree and I feel that no large garden, even though the owner might not be a magnolia nut, should be without it.

From the large Asiatic magnolias that are scented, you could grow what many consider one of the most beautiful magnolias, that is *Magnolia sprengeri* 'Diva' (zones 7–9). Also called the goddess magnolia, it blooms a lovely clear pink. Also worthy are

the scented varieties 'Copeland Court' (pink) and 'Claret Cup' (a rosy purple).

Then, very different, and like 'Wada's Memory' (above) grown not only for its individual small, white, scented flowers but for its impact as a whole, is the species *Magnolia salicifolia* (zones 6–9), which is smothered in color for a very long period.

There is a cultivar of *Magnolia sargentiana* var *robusta* called 'Blood Moon' (zones 7–9) that has flowers in a crimson-purple that are heavenly scented. I do not yet own this treasure, but after seeing a photograph in J. M. Gardiner's *Magnolias: A Gardeners Guide* I want it in my garden. The color looks absolutely wonderful and to think that it is also scented.

The aristocratically bred 'Caerhay's Belle' is very strongly scented with beautiful, soft pink flowers and I like the variety 'Sweetheart' even better (zones 6–9).

Dr. Todd Gresham's superb white magnolia 'Tina Durio' is sweetly scented.

Table of magnolias for perfume	Species or cultivar	Height x width	Hardiness zone
It is surprisingly difficult to narrow one's choice to ten with so many delectable varieties available. However, the following magnolias will all fill your garden with wonderful perfume.	M. 'Apollo'	40 x 20 ft (12 x 6 m)	6–9
	M. 'Athene'	30 x 15 ft (10 x 5 m)	6–9
	M. *denudata*	30 x 30 ft (10 x 10 m)	6–9
	M. x *loebneri* 'Leonard Messel'	25 x 20 ft (8 x 6 m)	5–9
	M. 'Milky Way'	30 x 15 ft (10 x 5 m)	6–9
	M. 'Pristine'	20 x 6 ft (6 x 1.8 m)	6–9
	M. 'Sayonara'	25 x 15 ft (6 x 5 m)	6–9
	M. 'Snow White'	10 x 12 ft (3 x 4 m)	6–9
	M. 'Sweetheart'	50 x 30 ft (15 x 10 m)	6–9
	M. 'Tina Durio'	20 x 15 ft (6 x 5 m)	6–9
	M. 'Vulcan'	30 x 10 ft (10 x 3 m)	6–9

CHAPTER 15

Family Connections

The Handsome Cousins

Liriodendron

Long before I realized that the *Liriodendron* is related to magnolias, I regarded it very highly, and I still do. This large, stately, deciduous tree comes from the eastern United States and has very interesting leaves. Not only are they a pleasant green, but they are truncated—the ends are squared off—which is surprisingly attractive. In the fall, the leaves turn a most attractive gold, a wonderful contrast to the reds, oranges and russets of many other deciduous trees.

You need to plan space for this tree that can very rapidly reach a height of 60 ft (18 m). It is the most pleasing pyrimidal shape, and in order to see its full beauty it should not be planted too cozily with other trees.

Its botanical name is *Liriodendron tulipifera*, hence its common name of tulip tree. As so often with this type of description, you need to give your imagination free rein. Yes, it does have a flower, but do not hold your breath waiting for this, because the tree has to be "mature" before this happens, and that takes about 12–15 years. The flower is a modest, greenish-yellow in color with an orange base, and is hidden by the tree's large leaves. But you do not grow this tree for its flowers, they are just a bonus on top of the beautiful leaves and fall color. Liriodendrons will grow in any reasonable soil that does not dry out and over a wide range of hardiness zones, 5–9.

A rather smaller-growing form (25–40 ft/8–12 m) called *Liriodendron tulipifera* 'Aureomarginata' has a lovely variegated leaf. The color is a sort of

The large stately North American tree *Liriodendron tulipifera* is a handsome relation of the magnolia.

blue-green with lemon-yellow margins and the leaves are square-ended. Colin Hutchinson's book *The Art of Gardening* calls it "a sophisticated tree in very good taste." You can't have a higher recommendation than that.

Although it has to be admitted that the *Liriodendron* is not always suitable for small gardens, it is another North American treasure.

Michelia doltsopa 'Silver Cloud' has gorgeous, large, scented flowers.

Michelia

Despite its smaller flowers, *Michelia* should not be considered a "poor relation" of the magnolia. From eastern Asia, there are close to fifty species, but almost all of these are tropical. Those that can grow in warm temperate and sub-tropical climates (zones 8–11) are limited in number but not in beauty. These trees or shrubs are evergreen, which certainly has its advantages, and are very floriferous. They flower all along the stems at the leaf axils, rather than at the end of the branches like the Asiatic magnolias.

I know personally of just three species, but even as I write, there is work being done on hybridizing these rather delightful plants. Mark Jury of New Zealand has been experimenting with various crosses for some years.

Michelia doltsopa is an absolutely splendid tree that grows quite tall (32 ft/10 m) and is very touchy about frost, especially the flowers. Its hardiness is rated as zones 8–9, so if you can do grow it. It is not only a very handsome evergreen with lovely shining green leaves, it has the most beautifully scented, creamy colored flowers. A *Michelia* in full bloom, which happens in the early spring, scents the air for many feet all around. It looks a bit like a decorated Christmas tree, except that all the decorations are white.

Duncan and Davies Nursery of New Plymouth, New Zealand, have introduced a variety called 'Silver Cloud' that flowers when very young with the most amazing number of flowers, so much so that I find it politic to remove some of the spent flowers to relieve the branches of the weight.

Not only are the *Michelia doltsopa* flowers both beautiful and scented, but the long, bright russet buds are a real delight. I especially like this extra dimension. Trees of the magnolia family have extraordinarily beautiful buds, so full of promise, that even in the winter you have something to contemplate that is visually very pleasing.

The so-called port wine michelia is the species *Michelia figo*, which is a small, frost-tender (zone 9), evergreen tree with creamy yellow flowers flushed reddish-purple. The flowers hang modestly downward. The real attraction of the tree is its very strong fragrance, which has been likened to port wine, hence the common name. It has been suggested, because it is tender, that it could be grown in a pot, but it would need to be a large pot, otherwise, without planning to, you would probably find yourself with a bonsai specimen.

The third species with which I am familiar, and for which I have a particular affection, is *Michelia yunnanensis* (zones 8–10), which comes from China. It is a bushy, quite fast-growing shrub (10 ft/3 m) absolutely smothered in small, fragrant, white flowers. It is very pretty, flowering later than the others, and so less liable to incur damage from frost. It can also be grown as a very attractive hedge.

I hope that we will be able to look forward to a greater selection of michelia in the future and this is a welcome thought for, especially in the small garden, this genus has much to offer.

Epilogue

I have greatly enjoyed writing this book, so I hope that you as readers have found some pleasure in it. I decided that, having thought about, studied and lived with magnolias for many months, I would have some fun as a finale. I thought it would wonderfully concentrate my ideas if I decided which magnolias that I simply would not live without (at least until such time as my family pop me into an old folks' home).

These fabulous magnolias I will limit to twenty, otherwise, I fear I might just make a long list of every one that I have mentioned in the previous pages.

1. *Magnolia* x *loebneri* 'Leonard Messel' (pages 65, 81). First, I absolutely adore it for its lovely, profuse, star-like flowers in soft lilac pink. To be beautiful, of course, flowers do not have to be large and they are not on this magnolia. Then the flowers are scented and what's more, and I think this important, they are cold-hardy (zone 5). In the fall, surprisingly for most magnolias, the leaves turn a very pleasing yellow. A further virtue, if one were needed, is that it is small enough to fit into almost any garden.

2. Felix Jury's 'Vulcan' (pages 44–45, 69, 82). It has its faults when immature (see page 45), but as a mature tree its color is a splendid red-purple and its medium-sized flowers have a delicate shape and poise that is most pleasing. The tree itself is nicely slender.

Magnolia × *loebneri* 'Leonard Messel'

Above: *Magnolia campbellii* var *alba* 'Strybing White'
Right: 'Vulcan'

3. *Magnolia campbellii* var *alba* 'Strybing White' (pages 40, 55). It is different from other *campbellii*, as the outer tepals droop instead of forming the familiar "saucer". Some people do not care for this, but I think it most fetching. It is not its fault that it flowers so early in spring that it can be frosted, but I am prepared to take the risk that I won't rejoice in its flowers every year.

4. *Magnolia campbellii* subsp *mollicomata* 'Lanarth' (page 67). A quite incredible color of deep magenta red, that gradually fades as the flower ages. But that is of no consequence, as the emerging color is dramatic in the extreme. Nothing short of gorgeous.

5. *Magnolia campbellii* 'Darjeeling' (page 67). Another wonderful color, this time a more wine-like crimson purple. It has all the virtues of M. *campbellii*, but with a truly royal color.

6. 'Tina Durio' (pages 47, 58, 83). From the stable of the wonderful Dr. Todd Gresham, who bred so many beauties, this one is white, flushed with pink at the base, and scented. It is most desirable.

7. Jury's 'Apollo' (pages 45, 68–69, 82). A stunningly dark, violet purple on the outside, pink within.

8. 'Lotus' (pages 44, 58–59). A Jury hybrid, creamy colored with pink-flushed base, and truly the shape of a water lily when open. It is scented, too.

9. 'Caerhay's Belle' (pages 63, 84). Lovely, but even better, I like its seedling called 'Sweetheart', which is a rich pink outside and pale pink inside. Both are beautiful and generous.

10. *Magnolia denudata* (pages 55–56, 57, 82). Its blooms are pure white and scented, sitting upright along the branches.

11. 'Suishoren' (page 59). Similar to *Magnolia denudata* with white, scented, upright blooms, but smaller and daintier.

12. *Magnolia sprengeri* 'Diva' (pages 40, 61–62, 63, 68). Very well named, for it is a star. The color is a gorgeous dark pink with a hint of purple. This beauty is fragrant.

'Apollo'

14. 'Snow White' (pages 57, 82). A little beauty with neat, scented flowers on a small tree.

Above: 'Snow White'
Opposite: 'Sayonara'

15. 'Sayonara' (pages 47, 58, 83). A gorgeous Gresham hybrid with large, goblet-shaped, cream

'Ruby Star'

flowers flushed pink at the base and scented.

16. 'Manchu Fan' (pages 48, 58). Another Gresham, with rather smaller tulip-shaped white flowers, also with a pink base. I would just hate to be without either 'Sayonara' or 'Manchu Fan'.

17. *Magnolia cylindrica* (page 57). Very special. The tall flowers sit like candles, and they are pure white with characteristic reddish stripes running up the sides of the flowers. It has both grace and charm.

18. *Magnolia soulangeana* 'Alba' (syn 'Alba Superba') (pages 51–52, 59). Aptly named, this superb tree is both white, and did I say superb?

19. 'Milky Way' (pages 44, 62, 82). Another Jury hybrid white suffused with pink, with its flowers sitting proudly along the branches.

20. 'Ruby Star' (page 46). An as-yet unreleased Jury hybrid, its spectacular reddish-purple flowers stand tall upon the branches.

Useful Addresses

The importation of live plants and plant materials across borders requires special arrangements, which will be detailed in suppliers' catalogs.

American regulations vary according to the country of origin and type of plant. Every order requires a phytosanitary certificate and may require a CITES (Convention on International Trade in Endangered Species of Wild Fauna and Flora) certificate. For more information contact:
USDA-APHIS-PPQ
Permit Unit
4700 River Road, Unit 136
Riverdale, Maryland 20727-1236
Tel: (301) 734-8645
Fax: (301) 734-5786
Website: www.aphis.udsda.gov

Canadians importing plant material must pay a fee and complete an "application for permit to import."
Contact:
Plant Health and Production Division
Canadian Food Inspection Agency
2nd Floor West, Permit Office
59 Camelot Drive
Nepean, Ontario K1A 0Y9
Tel: (613) 225-2342
Fax: (613) 228-6605
Website: www.cfia-agr.ca

Angelgrove Tree Seed Company
P.O. Box 74, Riverhead
Harbour Grace, Newfoundland A0A 3P0
Website: www.tree-seeds.com
Mail order supplier of hardy magnolia seeds.

Arborvillage Farm Nursery
P.O. Box 227
Holt, Missouri 64048
Tel/Fax: (816) 264-3911
E-mail: Arborvillage@aol.com
Wide selection of magnolias. Catalog $1.00. Ships to Canada.

Camellia Forest Nursery
125 Carolina Forest Road,
Chapel Hill, North Carolina 27516
Tel: (919) 968-0504
Fax: (919) 960-7690
Website: www.camforest.com
Flowering shrubs and trees from China and Japan.

Eastern Plant Specialties
P.O. Box 226W
Georgetown, Maine 04548
Tel: (732) 382-2508
Website: www.easternplant.com
Catalog available. Selection of magnolia seedlings.

Forestfarm
990 Tetherow Road
Williams, Oregon 97544-9599
Tel: (541) 846-7269
Fax: (541) 846-6963
Website: www.forestfarm.com
Good selection of magnolias. Ships to Canada.

Fraser's Thimble Farms
175 Arbutus Road
Salt Spring Island, British Columbia V8K 1A3
Tel/Fax: (250) 537-5788
Website: www.thimblefarms.com
E-mail: thimble@saltspring.com
Specializes in rare magnolias. Order by fax or e-mail. Ships to U.S.

Gossler Farms Nursery
1200 Weaver Road
Springfield, Oregon 97478-9691
Tel: (541) 746-3922
Exotic and rare offerings. Emphasis on magnolias at moderate prices.

Greer Gardens
1280 Goodpasture Island Road
Eugene, Oregon 97401-1794
Tel: (541) 686-8266
Toll-free Tel: (800) 548-0111
Fax: (905) 686-0910
Website: www.greergardens.com
Good selection of magnolias. Ships to Canada.

Heronswood Nursery, Ltd.
7530 NE 288th Street
Kingston, Washington 98346
Tel: (360) 297-4172
Fax: (360) 297-8321
Website: www.heronswood.com
Selection of rare magnolias. Excellent catalog.

Klehm's Song Sparrow Perennial Farm
13101 E. Rye Road
Avalon, Wisconsin 53505
Tel: (800) 553-3715
Fax: (608) 883-2257
Website: www.klehm.com/www.songsparrow.com
Ornamental plants for the NorthAmerican climate. Ships to Canada.

Louisiana Nursery
5853 Highway 182
Opelousas, Louisiana 70570
Tel: (337) 948-3696
Fax: (337) 942-6404
Website: www.louisiananursery.org
Carries over 600 different varieties of magnolias. Full-color catalog. Not all magnolias are listed on website. Ships to Canada.

The Magnolia Society
Roberta Hagen, Secretary
6616 81st Street
Cabin John, Maryland 20818
Tel: (301) 320-4296

Fax: (301) 320-4296
Website: www.tallahassee.net/~magnolia
E-mail: Rhagen6902@aol.com
Publishes newsletters and journals, organizes seed exchanges and promotes cultivation of magnolias.

Molbak's
13625 N.E. 175 Street,
Woodinville, Washington 98072
Tel: (425) 483 5000
Website: www.molbaks.com
Wide range of plants and seeds.

Wayside Gardens
1 Garden Lane
Hodges, South Carolina 29695
Tel: (800) 213-0379
Website: www.waysidegardens.com
Magnolias in all colors.

Woodlanders
1128 Colleton Avenue
Aiken, South Carolina 29801
Tel/Fax: (803) 648-7522
Website: www.woodlanders.net
E-mail: woodland@triplet.net
Over 1000 rare and exotic plants, specializing in southeastern native plants.

Yucca Do Nursery
P. O. Box 907
Hempstead, Texas 77445
Tel: (979) 826-4580
Website: www. yuccado.com
E-mail: info@yuccado.com
Plants for warm, dry climates.

Bibliography

Callaway, Dorothy J. *The World of Magnolias.* Portland: Timber Press, 1994.

Gardiner, J.M. (Jim). *Magnolias, A Gardener's Guide.* Portland: Timber Press, 2000.

Hunt, David (ed.) *Magnolias and their Allies.* London: International Dendrology Society, 1998.

Johnstone, G. H. *Asiatic Magnolias in Cultivation.* London: Royal Horticultural Society, 1955.

Rankin, Graham. *Magnolia, A Hamlyn Care Manual.* London: Hamlyn, 1999.

Treseder, Neil G. *Magnolias.* London: Faber & Faber, 1978.

Index